In Your Own Voice

"[A] very personal approach to writing. Puts the techniques together and effectively illustrates the valuable reserves of material provided by one's own life."
— *Writer's Digest* **praise for** *Writing From Within*

"Mr. Selling's techniques inspired considerable creativity among our creative staff and his feedback techniques are wonderful."
— **Peggy Van Pelt, Disney Imagineering**

"Bernard's method of teaching a person how to write a life story is just extraordinary. His feedback is not to be missed. My stories became instantly powerful with his guidance."
— **Micheline Lerner, widow of Allan Jay Lerner**

Films by Bernard Selling

The Flying Machine (from a story by Ray Bradbury)
Three Miraculous Soldiers (from a story by Stephen Crane)
First Year, A.D.

Books by Bernard Selling

Writing From Within: A Unique Guide to Writing Your Life's Stories

In Your Own Voice

Using Life Stories to Develop Writing Skills

BERNARD SELLING

with Jim Strohecker

Hunter House Inc., Publishers
P. O. Box 2914
Alameda CA 94501–0914

Library of Congress Cataloging-in-Publication Data

Selling, Bernard
In your own voice: using life stories to develop writing skills /
by Bernard Selling; with Jim Strohecker
p. cm.
ISBN 0-89793-127-0 : $14.95 (soft cover) — ISBN 0-89793-143-2 (spiral bound) : $22.95
1. English language—Rhetoric—Study and teaching. 2. Autobiography—
Authorship—Study and teaching. 3. I. Stroheker, Jim. II. Title.
PE1479.A88S45   1993
808'.042'07—dc20   93-19964

Project Editor: Lisa Lee   Production Manager: Paul J. Frindt
Cover design: Jil Weil Graphic Design   Book design: *Qalagraphia*
Copy Editors: Rachel Farber, Lynne Porter   Proofreader: Theo Crawford
Editorial Assistance: Jonathan Kromrey   Production Assistance: María Jesús Aguiló
Sales & Marketing: Corrine M. Sahli   Publicity & Promotion: Darcy Cohan
Customer Support: Sharon R.A. Olson, Sam Brewer
Order Fulfillment: A & A Quality Shipping Services
Publisher: Kiran S. Rana
Typeset in Palatino by 847 Communications, Alameda CA
Printed and bound by Malloy Lithographing, Ann Arbor MI

Manufactured in the United States of America

9   8   7   6   5   4   3   2   1   First edition

Ordering Information

Trade bookstores and wholesalers in the U.S. and Canada, please contact

Publishers Group West
4065 Hollis, Box 8843
Emeryville CA 94608
Telephone 1-800-788-3123 or (510) 658-3453
Fax (510) 658-1834

Special sales

Hunter House books are available at special discounts when purchased
in bulk for sales promotions, premiums, or fundraising.
For details, please contact

Special Sales Department
Hunter House Inc.
P.O. Box 2914
Alameda CA 94501–0914
Telephone (510) 865-5282
Fax (510) 865-4295

College textbooks/course adoption orders

Please contact Hunter House at the address and phone
number above.

Orders by individuals or organizations

Hunter House books are available through most bookstores or can be ordered
directly from the publisher by calling toll-free:

1-800-266-5592

To Will and Jeff, my sons

———————————————————

I'd reached the age of thirty-eight and wanted to assess my life—
figure out what had gone wrong, what had gone right.
I started at the beginning; I started with my first memory.
As soon as I remembered the first memory of my life,
everything started to flow.
— Sting

CONTENTS

Contents (continued)

FOREWORD

During the Spring of 1981, while serving as a Senior Fulbright Lecturer on Ethnic Studies at the University of Rome, I wrote an article for an emerging journal of literary criticism, MELUS (Multi-Ethnic Literature of the United States). It was a theoretical piece entitled "Cultural Consciousness—Its Uses in Literature."

In the article, I spoke to the processes through which all the immigrant and migrant groups that came to North America found their collective cultural voices in order to assert their presences on the continent. From the earliest and deepest voices of the various indigenous peoples to the latest immigrants from Asia, Latin America, and Eastern Europe, all of our cultural voices have made their discrete and separate sounds, and, over time, have affected and commingled with each other. The processes are ongoing, constantly changing, always dynamic, never static. If Caucasian voices dominated American Literature through the middle of the twentieth century, we must remember that during that time African Americans, Native Americans, Asians, Hispanics, and others were preserving their cultures for emergence and reemergence. At the beginning of the twenty-first century, the sounds of America's voices will be very much different from what they were at the beginning of the twentieth century—much more diverse, much more multicultural, much more interesting and compelling to a diverse global community. The world's peoples have come to America and have juxtaposed their cultures and sometimes have bridged cultural identities to articulate new sounds and new entities. Such "bridging" can emerge only when the cultures doing the "bridging" are confident in their own discrete identities and understand the unique and universal values in all cultural heritages, including those with which they are commingling.

When I first met Bernard Selling, eighteen years before I wrote the "Cultural Consciousness" article, we were in our early twenties and both teaching literature at the University level. We have taken quite separate routes since then—mine a more traditional career in academia, his in music, filmmaking, and writing. Yet, when I read his first book, *Writing From Within*, I realized that his interest in individual life stories closely paralleled my interest in the lives of cultural groups. Then, when I read *In Your Own Voice*, I recognized more fully that the composite of his microcosms formed my macrocosm.

In order for both cultures and individuals to flourish, they must believe in the continuum of people who, through time, have produced, biologically and culturally, their present. They must appreciate the value of their collective and individual pasts in order to compete in an increasingly complex world. It strikes me that *In Your Own Voice* will encourage individuals to do just that. For, in recognizing the value of one's own life, by extension, one recognizes the value of the lives of people like oneself, and then, by further extension, the value of the lives of people different from oneself. Confidence in one's own culture should be the first condition for appreciating and understanding others and exploring underlying similarities embodied in our rich variety.

This book should find its place in urban settings and in all parts of the country where multi-ethnic majorities are emerging. Mr. Selling is correct when he states that ignoring the tradition of individual and group storytelling "is one reason why Blacks and Latin immigrants have a great deal of trouble in our educational system: each has a long and noble tradition of storytelling which is not valued by the dominant white Anglo culture." One can easily add Native Americans as well.

In Your Own Voice encourages students to find their own voices and confidently express their thoughts and feelings, but not as an end in itself. As Selling states:

> "Those who explore their experiences through life story writing are in a much better position to commence analytic work than those who do not. There are similarities in the opening (teaser, question thesis), narrative (summary), dialogue (quotes), climax (analysis), denouement (conclusion) . . . "

Yet each way of perceiving promotes understanding, reflection, tolerance, and objectivity in understanding the events of the world around us—our own small world of experience and the larger universe of experience that surrounds us, often out of sight but not out of mind.

Learning to understand one's own voice is the first step in knowing all things. Emerson knew that. Thoreau knew that every person should be able to explain where he or she lived and what they lived for. *In Your Own Voice* can encourage such understanding in everyone who embraces it, strengthening and enhancing each individual's capacity to find success in a complex and competitive world.

Wayne C. Miller
Dean of Arts and Sciences,
University of Alaska Anchorage

Wayne Miller has written eight books dealing with American cultural change. In addition to his scholarly work he has written and produced 60 hours of prime-time PBS television and has served as a university administrator and corporate manager.

PREFACE

The "Writing from Within" process began taking shape when I was asked to lead a senior citizen's class in life story writing in the San Fernando Valley in the early 1980s. They discovered ways of leaving powerfully written stories to following generations while having the opportunity to review the lives they had lived, acknowledging their strengths and forgiving themselves for their weaknesses. Its success encouraged me to develop similar classes in various parts of Los Angeles and to begin training other teachers to do the same.

I began teaching my life story writing process as a workshop at Antioch University in Marina del Rey. Bright, young (and not so young) college students oriented toward psychology found it to be a profound experience of getting to know themselves better while gaining skills and techniques which enhanced their academic and creative writing. At the same time, a few teachers—most of them in the Los Angeles Unified School District—discovered this approach to writing and asked me to work with them to make writing easier and more interesting for their students.

These teachers and administrators, working primarily with disadvantaged and remedial students, found that their students responded dramatically to the opportunities being given them. In writing their earliest vivid memories, reading their work aloud, then getting enthusiastic feedback from their classmates, these students found their writing abilities developing rapidly and their sense of self-worth increasing at a like pace. Most of all, they enjoyed themselves. A tough and demanding chore had become a pleasure. I would like to thank these dedicated teachers, administrators, parents and grandparents, in particular Andrew Siegenfeld, Lynne Porter, Roz Goldstein, and Stella Goren in Los Angeles and Janet Ford in North Carolina, for their efforts in bringing this approach to the young.

Finally, I would like to thank Jim Strohecker for his invaluable help, particularly in the formative stages of this book. His enthusiasm for the purposes of the book, his exceptional ability to provide feedback about and a context for the ideas explored, as well as his acuity in defining what the readers would want to know, led to this book becoming a reality in a much shorter time than would otherwise have been possible.

I hope you will find this method as helpful to you and your students as I have found it to be in helping myself and others "write from within."

In Your Own Voice

INTRODUCTION

*"The United States in the 1980s may be the first society in history
in which children are distinctly worse off than adults."*
— Sen. Daniel Moynihan

One of our nation's greatest concerns is the future of its children. Our society is bombarded daily with concerns about child abuse, child care, child education, child violence and the like. How to help the gifted child excel, cope, relate, absorb, and contribute is one set of concerns. How to enable the child to grow to adulthood without being stunted by the often painful demands of growing up is another.

Our society recognizes that childhood is a stage of life during which the child must be protected from harm while absorbing the positive values of the adult society around it. And our society is beginning to recognize that it is failing on both counts: the child is not being protected from harm and is not absorbing the positive values of American society. "How do we reverse this process?" we ask.

Recovering Childhood as a State of Mind

Childhood—being a child—is more than a stage of life; it is also a state of mind. It is a state of mind in which the world is fresh and seen with new eyes, just as the child's responses are new and dramatic. As a stage of life, it is something most of us wanted to get through quickly and become adults; as a state of mind, it is something most of us treasured and lost, a loss most of us continue to rue forever. Many of us never even know childhood as a state of mind.

Fortunately, a number of public figures in the healing arts—Alice Miller, John Bradshaw, Lucia Capacchione, and Charles Whitfield among them—have recognized the importance of recovering the child existing in us all as an experience and as a state of mind *and of continuing that state into and throughout adulthood.*

One contemporary school of psychotherapy holds that if our parents were unkind or unresponsive or in any way not what we wanted or needed, we must then recreate our parents in our minds and hearts the way we need them to be; i.e., reparent ourselves in order to be high-functioning people. A corollary is the need to recover, as well, the child within as a state of mind *and maintain that state throughout the remainder of our lives.*

Most people . . . would admit that the English language is in a bad way, but it is generally assumed that we cannot by conscious action do anything about it [as if] language is a natural growth and not an instrument which we shape for our own purposes . . . .

— George Orwell
*Politics and the
English Language*

1

What is it that the indwelling child offers us as we move into adult life? The child is the fount of play, endless creation, experimentation, and discovery. The child sees and hears things for the first time and names them in unique ways. Childhood as a state of mind feels safe from the cares and pain of actuality. Childhood is feeling that each moment is a step into an unknown, into a world created by magic, but of uncertainty from which one can retreat to the safety of loving parents.

Many visual artists of the twentieth century are well ahead of the rest of us in recognizing and entering into childhood as a state of mind. Paul Klee, Joan Miro, Jean Arp, Alexander Calder, Henri Matisse, and Pablo Picasso have entered the child's world of playful images, spontaneity, and innocence and enriched our lives with the results.

Those of us for whom childhood is not a present state of mind but a past stage of development are inclined to recollect it as a time to be avoided, forgotten, or dismissed. It was a time of embarrassment, pain, subservience, discipline, and obedience. The less said about it the better.

Best of all is the gift of immaturity itself, which has enabled us to retain in our most human moments, the capacity for play.

— Joseph Campbell
*Masks of God:
Primitive Mythology*

Some of the most perceptive commentators on society, such as Carl Jung, Abraham Maslow, and Robert Bly, remind us that the healthy individual (and the larger society) must carry within the play element—the "homo ludens" or "childhood as a state of mind"—throughout life. Our zest for life, our willingness to confront the unknown, our appreciation for "the trickster" in our lives, depends on it.

Because we live in a serious age, we seem to value those who conduct their business skillfully but irreverently. William Buckley playing with words, Picasso playing with pictures, Magic Johnson playing with a basketball, and Louis Armstrong playing with music intrigue us.

Preserving childhood as a state of mind over the course of a lifetime is a challenge. Few of us understand how easily a child can be damaged or pushed off his or her natural track. For close to a decade I have worked with senior citizens whose task has been to recover their childhoods. During that time I have heard countless stories recollecting birth to six months old. Despite the lack of language in infancy, there often exists a clear recall of events. This work reminds me of the importance of being good to children: what they see, even in infancy, will remain with them all their lives.

The "Critic" vs. Childhood as a State of Mind

Another force that assaults childhood as a state of mind is the onset of the "critic" in the lives of virtually everyone. Like a jealous god, it dismisses and even tries to vanquish all that has come before it. Childhood as a state of mind is tender and easily intimidated, so it hides itself. Even when most needed in life, it hides in fear of the awesome power of the critic.

Considerable research has been conducted about the two sides of the brain. The right side is responsible for visualizing things, synthesizing, and seeing the "all at once." Out of the right brain arises the creator, the trickster, and Dionysus—all vestiges of child-hood play.

The left side takes care of other functions: analyzing things, using language to communicate, creating abstract symbols to stand for things, learning in a step-by-step manner. The critic is the cau-tionary voice. It sits atop the left side of the brain and legislates what we should and should not do. It is the cautionary voice that helps guide us out of trouble and down a path of independent activity that is safe and sane. It is the voice of reason, the voice of Apollo.

Most people tend in one direction or another. They live out of their left brains, doing analytical work with a rather rational stance toward life or else throw caution to the wind with a right-brain freedom. The real task of adult life is to integrate these two voices: the voice of caution and the voice of creation.

The critical voice that dominates the working lives of most people from the teens on begins to relax when we reach our sixties. If we have planned properly, we look forward to the retirement that affords us the opportunity to reflect on the lives we have led. From this state of reflection comes a wonder at what we have been through. Childhood as a state of mind begins to emerge once again. From the ruminations of St. Augustine to the present, however, the looking-backwards process has been a process of viewing the changeable past from the unchanging perspective of the "elder" looking backward. Somehow we need to find a way to allow the child's voice to speak from the past as if it were the present moment.

Recovering the Authentic Child's Voice in Our Writing

My work in the theater with the Stanislavski method of transforming the actor into a character "in the moment" persuaded me to seek ways of enabling the backward-looking autobiographer to do more than just look at the past. He or she needs to be "in" the past.

From this effort has come a systematic process for recovering the voice of the child, a voice which has lain under the accretion of adult voices for so long that we no longer hear our most intimate and innocent voice. In this child's voice we find our own authentic voice that enables us to cast our experiences in intimate, vivid, simple, and emotional language. It enables us to tell our stories in such a way that children understand and trust us. It enables us to get out of our adult selves and into ourselves at another time and place, to write of experiences not as though they were a long way off—as if at the end of a tunnel—but as if we are "in" the experience. It is the voice of the storyteller.

Writing our life stories in this way gives us the opportunity to approach events and experiences both truthfully and creatively. We learn that writing is not a thing so magical that only a few can do it. Each one of us can create. We can write. How do we do this? By softening our critic, seeking out helpful feedback, and becoming aware of our own process when we work, we discover our own authentic voices as writers and can help our children do the same.

First, we teachers and parents need to begin looking at life through the innocent eyes of the child. We can do this by learning how to strip away our old adult writing voice and discover the child within. In doing so, we can write stories that are fresh, direct, visual, and emotional, and we can teach others to do the same.

Then we begin to help the child find his or her own "authentic child's voice" that captures the vividness of the child's experience. If we can discover and nourish that voice in the child, then the next step is to keep that authentic voice alive as the child gets older and becomes more self-critical. If it is the older child whom we are teaching, we need to help that child get past his or her own critic and discover the authentic child's voice within.

If we are searching for an "authentic child's voice" in the child and in ourselves, does that mean there is an "unauthentic child's voice" to be overcome? The answer is both yes and no. Yes, there is an opposite to "authentic" and no, the term is not "unauthentic." The appropriate term is probably "unformed." The younger child carries around vivid memories of experiences inside himself or herself. By the time the child is in the third or fourth grade, he or she has sufficient language to express a great deal of this experience. But the child needs to be shown how language and experience connect. That is the task of *In Your Own Voice.*

If left to her or his own devices, the child will become more articulate, but often less authentic. Why is this? For the most part, teachers try to help the maturing child become more adult. The effort in this book is to assist you in helping the child become articulate *and* authentic, keeping the child's voice alive.

By the time the child has become a teenager, the child's voice has, for the most part, been lost. The leap from childhood to adulthood has been painful, without rites of passage, or the assistance of elders, as Robert Bly would put it. As a college English and humanities teacher for over thirty years, I found most students unable to write simple, direct, clear statements. One of the tasks of this book is to help the teenager recover that child's voice and form her or his own "authentic writer's voice."

How does this stress on "authentic" personal writing help the college-bound writer deal with analytical and research papers? Since there is a strong connection between the two, I have included a chapter on writing analytical papers, which compares and contrasts the two.

Education and Childhood as a State of Mind

For the better part of the twentieth century two traditions in education have vied for supremacy. Traditional education, modeled on the English school system, holds the standard that we should imitate the great works of the past. Reading literature, writing modeled on this literature, and doing arithmetic soon follow. This tradition often assumes a view of humanity that is consistent with the dominant religious values of Western thought: a fall from a state of grace and an inherently bad, evil, ignorant, self-gratifying self that must be disciplined to behave in a humane, civilized way.

The second tradition, following the teachings of John Dewey and William James, encourages the child to explore the world with minimal interference from the teacher, believing that the powerful inner urge to know and the powerful impact of one's peer group will create a child filled with curiosity and unfettered by stultifying ideas. This approach assumes the child is, like Rousseau's natural man, both good and wise and he or she needs only to be left alone to unfold.

A third tradition exists in many peasant and "primitive" societies: the tradition of storytelling. The values of great and good heroes, as well as errant and mischievous gods, are embodied in stories that captivate and teach at the same time. These values are conveyed wonderfully in the work of Joseph Campbell, notably in *The Hero With a Thousand Faces* and *The Masks of God*. Regrettably, this tradition has been all but ignored in American education. It is one reason why Native Americans, African Americans, and many immigrant groups have a great deal of trouble in our educational system: each has a long and noble tradition of storytelling that is not valued by the dominant white culture.

There is some hope on the horizon. Theater, which so often carries on this tradition of storytelling, has had a growing impact on education over the past twenty years. In Los Angeles, for example, the Los Angeles Theater Center has an extensive in-school educa-

Since the period of the Renaissance, we of the West have come to believe that the proper aim of education is the inculcation of information about the world in which we live . . . [but] This, however, was not the aim in the past, nor is it the aim, in the orient. In primitive, archaic and oriental spheres [it] has always been and will no doubt continue to be to create communities of shared experience for the engagement of the sentiments of the growing individual in matters of chief importance to the local group.

Joseph Campbell
Masks of God: Primitive Mythology

tional program in which the voices of minority cultures, the homeless, and the disenfranchised may be heard.

"Writing from within" may be seen, in part, as an effort to return storytelling to its rightful place at the center of a child's education—not storytelling that is just airy imagining (somewhat akin to lying, a conservative might say) but storytelling that allows the child to use the most vivid experiences of his or her life to better understand himself or herself and the world outside.

Many educators take the position that the purpose of education is to turn the child into an adult. Certainly it is the position taken by conservatives in education. The liberal wing tends to want to leave the child alone to flourish. Neither is on track. In education, as in business and many other areas, we as a nation polarize. Some go left toward the liberal side of the body politic and the right brain's free-flowing functions; others go right, toward the cautious side of the body politic and the left brain's analytical functions. Education ought to allow us access to both. It should help each of us find our most natural mode of expression and learning.

This nation's educational system does take writing very seriously. Recently there has been a strong movement toward something called literature-based writing. Embedded in this approach is the notion that adults have much to teach children: by knowing literature—and writing about it—the child will learn how to write as adults do. Unfortunately, learning to write does not really work this way. Our earliest voice is narrative, not analytical. The child who reads literature in order to write loses his or her own valuable inner voice in the process. Experience shows that the child (as well as the adult) who is encouraged to find his or her own authentic, inner voice becomes excited about writing and then becomes excited about reading and literature.

The first evidence of writing found in the sands of the ancient Middle East tells us that learning to write did not come from first learning to read. Writing occurred from the need to store information about the day's events, stories of family life, and, later, feelings. Then came reading—so that this writing could be shared.

Adults have much to learn from children about writing. The best thing we as adults can do is to honor the child's voice within us all. It is the purpose of this book to guide each of us to our own voices.

The Inner City and Childhood as a State of Mind

The ghettos and barrios of this country are filled with young children who can learn but do not, turning instead to sex, drugs, rap, and rock. Why? Can they be gotten back on track? Can this writing method help them?

During the late 1960s and early 1970s I explored these problems in a series of documentary films I made in East Los Angeles. One young man whom I followed for several years was beset by family problems: the death of his Mexican father, the alcoholism of his Native American mother, a brother in prison. He was a sensitive, intelligent boy who soon dropped out of school and began a long involvement with drugs and the law.

As I got to know him better over the years I followed him around and then got to know a number of other youngsters in an East Los Angeles job training program, one thing became clear: children in poverty have enormous problems weighing on them all the time. Life is filled with an endless series of mini-dramas. Each problem becomes a reason to stay away from school, a place that has none of the drama of the streets.

"What can be done to keep kids like this in school?" I asked myself. "Can the problems be diminished? Can schools become more interesting, more relevant?" At the time I thought that a constellation of caring adults was the answer—teachers who understood their students and communicated to parents who talked to social workers who talked to police officers.

Now, twenty-five years later, I ask the question differently: "What can the school do to help the youngster find a path through the dramas of a young, unsafe life? What role can the process of writing from within play in the lives of these children?"

For one thing, life story writing, and more particularly writing from within, allows children to explore the one thing they know really well—their own lives. It permits them to view and review, to recognize that family arguments can become the basis for well-observed stories and emotional release, and to see that those "bad dudes who are rappin' on [his] head" are characters who make a story interesting reading. Furthermore, this writing process allows the child to use street language (dialogue) and school language (narrative and inner thoughts and feelings) at the same time, instead of asking them to discard a very real part of their lives when they enter school grounds.

For those students who are limited in their use of English, writing from within encourages the use of simple vocabulary in a powerful, immediate way. This command of language and feeling will feed their self-esteem and may well affect their future learning in a very positive way.

Emotional Health and Childhood as a State of Mind

This approach to life story telling is both an approach to writing and to creating improved emotional health. In our culture, unfortunately, storytelling carries little weight in our educational and child-rearing programs. Storytelling is thought of as inventing, and construed as close to lying.

Writing is and always has been the natural outlet for contemplating one's circumstances. "Writing from within" gives children the tools to dig deeply into their own circumstances and to develop awareness of themselves and the world around them. The stress on narrative, dialogue, and the expression of inner thoughts and feelings corresponds to the development of the child's sense of self. Starting at the center of the universe, they begin to view the world outside the self as fascinating and important, and then move inward again to the world of thought and feeling, which develops most strongly in the teenage years.

This approach to life story telling helps children grasp actual experience as well as invented experience. This kind of storytelling allows children to know and to accept their own world not as a pale imitation of the adult world, but as a rich, funny, touching, scary world of its own.

The "writing from within" process makes it possible for everyone with a rudimentary knowledge of English—from the child of the barrio, to the immigrant, the refugee, the homeless person, and the college graduate—to develop awareness of herself or himself and communicate that understanding to others by means of the simple, dignified, expressive language of the child that exists in us all. In the end, the process yields not only self-understanding but an artistic product about which each author can feel quite wonderful.

The beauty of the method is that, in its simplicity, it applies to all writers from the fourth grade on. Everyone going to the mountain rides the same train: younger writers get off at an earlier station; older writers go on. (We will find that young and old, in this sense, are not chronological terms but psychological ones)

As teachers and parents we can hope, quite legitimately, that the kind of examination of lives and values that goes on in "writing from within" will assist children in avoiding paths that lead to despair.

This book is dedicated to childhood as a state of mind: to helping children value and express it and to helping adults recover and express it. For the person who finds it, nourishes it, recovers it, and keeps in touch with it, writing from the authentic voice within is an inexhaustible source of self-worth and self-understanding.

Journaling and Other Approaches to Writing and Childhood as a State of Mind

The approach to writing that you will learn in this book is a new and quite different approach to writing. It is not in conflict, however, with the effective methods currently used in schools and personal growth classes, such as those that focus on journaling with the creative child within.

The approach of "writing from within" may be seen as picking up where the journaling approach ends. "Writing from within" allows the child or adult who has explored childhood as a state of mind for the purposes of healing and self-understanding to extend that understanding in self-expression. This process allows the writer to find in the voice of one's child within, an authentic writer's voice and to become confident in sharing with others who that child within is. "Writing from within" also allows any writer to grasp and express the dimensions of the outer world without losing the quality of prizing one's feelings gained in the journaling process.

Another significant benefit of "writing from within" occurs in helping the writer develop the capacity to understand relationships by portraying people and events and by discovering one's own responses to the actions and attitudes of others. "Drama," said Elia Kazan, director of *On the Waterfront* and *Streetcar Named Desire*, "is turning psychology into action." In this sense, we are discovering the drama of the child within by turning psychology into action.

Writing in a diary has always been a tool for understanding and remembering experiences. The great benefit of journaling has been to urge those who would write in their diaries to leave the world of fact behind and give free rein to that internal world of impulse and feeling. "Writing from within" similarly encourages the writer to step into the world of feelings and inner thoughts, while at the same time solidifying his or her grasp of the world of facts and relationships.

Writing one's autobiography has often meant writing down the facts of one's life without recording any feelings to accompany that experience. "Writing from within" enables the writer to build feelings, awareness, and the drama of relationships into the fabric of one's recollections.

Another popular approach to writing is what we call creative writing or fictional writing. Books such as Natalie Goldberg's *Writing Down the Bones* provide many practical as well as imaginative ways of accomplishing creative writing. There is behind every effort to do creative writing, however, the specter of those who have gone before, the giants of fiction writing—the Joyces and the Manns and the Hemingways and the O'Conners—standing over our shoulders evaluating our progress. It is tough to operate in such a ball park without feeling entirely out of one's league. "Writing from within" allows us to explore creativity and to use techniques of the fiction writer without feeling in any way in competition with these writers. The subject matter is one's own life and no one knows that life better than we do.

Overcoming the Fear of Writing

For many of us, putting our thoughts and feelings down on paper causes great anxiety. Whether we are teachers, students, or even writing professionals, the fear is there.

It took me many decades to understand and harness my own fears of writing. As the son of a highly-educated, psychiatrist/author father, I was accustomed to thinking independently from an early age. Writing lengthy term papers, even in junior high school, was not daunting, but I shied away from personal and creative writing. Although I read widely, I couldn't imagine actually writing about myself or making up fictional characters. "Nobody wants to hear about you and your opinions," my teachers would say to my classmates and me in school. "Don't get self-absorbed." I got the message: "You are not important." Likewise, my father, a man of science, was objective about almost everything. I assumed these authorities were right. I was not important and the only valuable writing was impersonal writing.

Then, when I was sixteen, my father died. I found myself wanting to hide from everyone and everything. I turned away from all the things I enjoyed doing—music, athletics, dating. I had no one to turn to and no means for expressing my aloneness."

As I began my career as a college writing teacher in my early twenties, I tried writing creatively, but I would always begin correcting whatever I had written a page or two into the story. The story idea would then slip away and I would give up. This pattern repeated itself for several years. Finally, I gave up trying to write in a creative way.

After a few years of teaching college, I went into the film industry and directed documentaries and short fiction films. I began studying the art of directing actors under the guidance of Lee Strasberg of the Actor's Studio. What a joy that was! In working with the actors' imaginations, I could create endlessly. My self-critic slept and my innermost, creative self opened up and poured out all kinds of imaginative personal experiences that helped the actors do their work.

Several years into this career, I began wondering if I might be able to harness my self-critic and perfectionist techniques and try

Language becomes ugly and inaccurate because our thoughts are foolish, but the slovenliness of our language makes it easier for us to have foolish thoughts. [Nevertheless], the process is reversible.

— George Orwell
Politics and the English Language

writing again. Slowly I began to realize that much of my difficulty stemmed from not wanting to deal with my own intimate, personal feelings on paper. I hid behind "perfect" beginnings and objective writing. My fears of revealing myself and my childhood pain stopped me from placing myself "onstage" in my own work; I still wanted to be as invisible as when my father died.

I looked around and saw I was not alone. My college writing students as well as my adult autobiographical writing students were immensely fearful of writing. Most thought they had to learn all the grammar and sentence structure possible before they dared to attempt any writing. They were terrified of being judged and criticized either for what they were saying or for the way they were saying it.

Gradually I began to see a way past all this fear: I could engage my students in personal writing as a prelude to doing academic writing and encourage them to explore memories of themselves in their childhoods *before* their highly critical, adult selves could take hold. I found that in exploring these early memories, my students and I were able to get in touch with strong pictures and feelings from the past. These moments became more and more vivid as we expressed the memories in small, simple, active words and short, powerful sentences. This way of writing seemed to strike close to the heart of the reader who was able to see pictures of people in the stories, hear their words, and feel their feelings. The writers appeared quite able to create these stories and feel safe from the powerful critics in themselves and others. Readers were touched, moved, and delighted as the writers began to find their own, authentic voices, which sounded much like the language of modern novels, plays, and movies.

I was delighted and intrigued to see that many of my students with modest English skills actually did better at this kind of personal writing than did more highly educated students who had to learn to let go of the impersonality and objectivity that hid their deepest feelings. I began to reflect on my own life, realizing that for most of my life I also hid behind my facility with words, never quite revealing my fears, uncertainties, embarrassments, and moments of sadness or weakness. "You are not important," my teachers and father had said.

I was even more delighted to see that the confidence and skill gained in doing personal writing carried over into academic and analytical writing. Once my students learned how to communicate from their hearts to the hearts of others, learning how to communicate head to head was no longer so daunting. They found the process of doing a research or analytical paper to be similar in many ways to the process of doing personal writing: finding a place and time to write, brainstorming to find a subject, beginning to write by exploring a vivid experience, rewriting to make the line through the story/paper clear, adding dialogue/quotes to create vividness, and editing and proofing the final copy.

Moreover, the teaching of college writing was also changing. My colleagues and I were realizing that students needed to have a point of view about the material. Being able to think objectively was important, but having a connection to the material was important, too. All of this became much easier for the student who had explored himself or herself and his or her experiences in my life writing classes.

Helping students explore and develop writing skills through personal writing felt like the missing link for which I had been searching during all my years of teaching.

In the days, weeks, months, and years after my father's death, I was in a great deal of pain. Had a personal writing method like the one I have outlined here been available, I might have been helped a great deal. Vast numbers of students come to school every day with the same weighty concerns that I faced as a high-school student. They need to feel that their developing language, writing, and communications skills will help them deal with their feelings and concerns. Analytical writing can also help them develop an essential understanding of the world around them.

I like to think that, with this method at hand, students now have an avenue for deepening their understanding of themselves and the world they live in. Some years ago, a high-risk student of mine wrote a very touching story. She got a lot of positive feedback from the class about the impact of her writing. "It really touched me," was the response of most students. I asked her how it felt to be so well received. "I don't feel so alone," she replied. That single comment made my thirty years of teaching worthwhile.

How to Use *In Your Own Voice*

In Your Own Voice has been arranged so you can teach the writing process to your students in an effective way. I suggest you read through all three parts of the book before you begin teaching: Part One—The Writing Process, Part Two—How to Use the Process, and Part Three—Life Writing Selections. After you have looked over the book, I suggest you reread Chapters 1 and 2 of Part One and then begin your teaching with Chapter 3. Specific assignments for students can be found within and also at the end of each chapter beginning with Chapter 4.

In Part One, we will take you through the various steps of the "writing from within" process. Included is a chapter that defines the writing stages through which children evolve and how these stages relate to teaching "writing from within." Examples are provided so you can see how children from different backgrounds have seen their writing improve through each stage of the work. The actual teaching begins with Chapter 3.

Part Two contains some suggestions for approaching the teaching of this method, including the experiences of one teacher who used this method with "at risk" students in a rural setting. It may help you in your teaching to see what these experiences were like. Also in this section, we look at ways in which you can use this method of writing life stories as a first step in helping students do analytical writing tasks. It is particularly effective with "at risk" students because it uses skills students already have and strengthens their development.

Part Three contains samples of student work that you and your students may enjoy reading. For older students, I particularly commend Liz Kelly's story, "Tank Top," as an expression of what students of today so often feel. For a glimpse into the experience of a young Latino gang member, please see "A Sad Memory." This work also illustrates how a student can learn to write effectively by moving through three drafts of a story in a matter of minutes. "The Overhead Bridge" by Eddie White and "Leaving the Plantation" by Florence Mayweather are good examples of the voice of childhood kept alive in adult writing. These two stories also illustrate two Black Americans' experiences in the South during the 1920s and 30s.

From time to time, you may desire a fuller explanation of some of the terms used in this book. A glossary of terms follows Part Three—Life Writing Selections. Brief examples and definitions may also be found within the book and near the end of each chapter.

This manual is designed to be a self-contained teaching unit. However, additional support materials are available. Student workbooks are available from the author and curriculum guides will soon be available from Hunter House Inc., Publishers. For more information, please see the back of the book.

This teaching method has been used and tested mostly with children of junior and senior high-school age. Our preliminary efforts suggest that the method can be used with much younger children, but much more testing must go on before we can be conclusive about this. For those of you who are teachers of younger children and find yourself using this method effectively, we welcome your input for suggested assignments and approaches to the material. These suggestions will be incorporated into a curriculum guide to be published in the future.

PART ONE

The Writing Process

1

WHAT IS "WRITING FROM WITHIN"?

"It takes a long time to become young"
— Pablo Picasso

When I was a child, my mother would tuck me into bed at night and tell stories in the dark, making pictures with the tip of her lit cigarette to go with her stories. Her favorite was about a man who could spit around corners. It was a wonderful time, a time I had forgotten about until I sat down to write this chapter.

We envy those who can lean back, put their feet up, gaze out the window and then proceed to cast a spell over their listeners with their storytelling. Most of us never dreamed as children that we could become storytellers ourselves. Today, however, it is possible for almost any child who has a story to tell (and we all do) to get it down on paper by using the "writing from within" method.

"No, no," some of your students' parents might say, "I don't want my child to spend precious time daydreaming." In a way, stories are daydreams, although many of history's most enchanting stories are based on actual events. Dreaming, whether during the day or night, is an important part of the process we use for solving problems and understanding ourselves. Stories based on our own lives can bring us a wonderful sense of our own place in the world and can help us see and understand our relationships to those around us.

By creating stories, we learn to take center stage in our own lives.

The Well-Told Story

What are the characteristics of a well-told story? First of all, there is a quality of innocence or magic, as if the event is seen in a way that is different from the life we all know. There is usually a vivid beginning, with characters who struggle against something powerful that is holding them back from getting what they rightfully deserve. In a fairy tale, it would sound something like . . . "Once upon a time, in a land far away there was a handsome prince who had sought everywhere for the love he knew was somewhere in his kingdom . . . " Sometimes the story is of a person who will one day be the center of power (the king) but is now merely on the threshold, waiting, getting his or her life in order.

Whatever the prize awaiting the hero or heroine, there is usually another larger, less defined prize to be gained, such as self-knowledge, self-respect, or self-love. In some stories, the struggle of the central character stands for the struggle of a larger group of people to find refuge, knowledge, love, and understanding.

When stories strike a resounding chord in a great many listeners, they are often elevated to the level of myth. Joseph Campbell writes eloquently in *The Hero With a Thousand Faces* of the power of myth and the characteristic stages through which the mythic hero proceeds. The lives of King Arthur, Lancelot, Percival, Odysseus, and Ahab are the stuff of myth as are the stories of the lives of Jesus, Mohammed, and Buddha. The shape of their stories takes on a larger-than-life quality, while the historical events of their lives have often been lost in time. This is storytelling at its best.

Describing "Writing from Within"

"Writing from within" is a special kind of storytelling that uses the actual events of a person's life in the telling of the story. It enables the writer to record the most vivid moments of life so that the outer world of action, relationships, and events is balanced by the need to express the inner world of thoughts and feelings. In this approach, each storyteller finds her or his own "authentic writing voice," based on her or his own "authentic child's voice."

This kind of writing is not a recitation of facts, as is common in the usual autobiography, nor is it an inner journey so private that no one but the writer is permitted to experience it, as is the case with contemporary journaling. It is a balanced view of the inner world and the outer world and is meant to be shared with others.

The objective of any writer is to create a world of experience and then invite the reader into this world. It is most important for the writer to create in the reader a sense of belief in this world, what T. S. Eliot calls "the willing suspension of disbelief." All too often, writers do certain things that create distance between the reader and the experience. The objective of "writing from within" is to minimize this distance and to engage the reader in the writer's experience so that the reader believes the experience as fully as possible.

"Writing from within" takes the writer back to her or his earliest memories and allows her or him to experience these memories as if

Art is a fruit growing out of a man like a fruit out of a plant, like the child out of the mother.

— Man Ray
Diary

they are actually happening and to speak from the point of view of the child who experienced these events. In this way, some of the magic and wonder of storytelling is gained or regained.

Definitions

Before we go any further it may be helpful to define a few of the terms that will appear throughout this book. You will find a fuller explanation of these terms in the glossary at the back of the book.

Narrative is the unfolding of events in a way that holds the reader's interest. It is the story and tends to be an objective or factual recounting of that story.

Narrator is the voice through which the story is being told. The narrator may be the central character in the story, or an onlooker viewing events from outside the story. In fiction the narrator may be impersonal or even God-like, looking down at events from a great distance.

Point of view is the vantage point from which the story is being told. For example, during the nineteenth century, the point of view was most often God-like and impersonal. In the twentieth century, readers tend to believe a story only if we know from whose point of view we are viewing the action; that is, who the narrator is.

Central character is the person around whom the events in a story are woven. It is his or her struggle that concerns us. The central character may or may not be the narrator.

Person is the voice telling the story. It may be told in the first person ("I went to the market"), in the second person ("you went to the market"), or in the third person ("she went to the market"). Most fiction is written in the third person (he, she, or they), however, most effective life writing is done in the first person.

Tense or time is one of the three basic time periods in which to set the story: the past, the present, and the future. In life writing we choose to narrate the story in the present rather than the past tense. Why? Because using the present tense while going into the past allows us to recreate that moment as if it were happening now. It creates a wonderful leap in the imagination of the writer and the reader.

Distance or distancing effect is the feeling a reader has of being kept at arm's length from the events in the story and from the emotions of the central characters. Distance can be frustrating for the reader who wants to know and feel more about these events and characters. The past tense automatically creates a sense of distance. Too many adjectives or adverbs create distance. Intellectual and emotionless words create distance. Stiff, complicated sentences also create distance.

Intimacy, or emotional intimacy, is the experience of knowing what the characters think and feel, and of being able to see the events described so closely that the reader feels swept up in the action and feelings of the moment. Dialogue creates a sense of intimacy between the narrator and the other characters. Inner thoughts and feelings create a sense of knowing the narrator as if he or she were your own self.

Dialogue is what is spoken between two or more people. It will make any story more interesting. Believable dialogue is dialogue we can imagine the person saying.

Inner monologue, or inner dialogue, is the words spoken inside the central character's head to herself or himself. For example: "Dad watches television all during dinner. 'I bet he won't even notice if I sneak some ice cream,' I think to myself." Inner monologue adds great richness to any story.

Belief is the way most of us judge the truth of a story. If it sounds believable, we tend to accept it as true. One of the goals of almost any writer is to get the reader to accept the characters and events in a story as believable. Almost every reader comes to reading stories or watching stories on television with a certain disbelief. This is healthy. The job of the writer is to get the readers to suspend this natural disbelief, to help the reader enter the world the writer is creating and to keep the reader there for the duration of the story.

Balance: In good writing, we seek a balance of narrative, dialogue, and inner monologue. In this way, the writer can convey to the reader what is going on in the outer world of action and events and emotions and in the inner world of the central character's thoughts and feelings.

The outer world is the public world of people and events that exists outside of ourselves.

The inner world is the private world in which we all dwell much of the time. This world includes our joys, fears, and thoughts.

Self-criticism: In our inner world, we often send messages to ourselves that tell us we are wrong, foolish, misguided, imperfect, and the like. Finding fault with ourselves causes us to feel badly about ourselves and causes us to stop doing the things we are doing.

"Writing from Within": A Step-by-Step Guide

How do we write from within? There are basically eight steps that accomplish this goal. Here is a quick overview of each step. Throughout the book you will find each step defined and explained.

First of all, we as writers *select the most vivid moments* of our experience and *create pictures* in our minds of the experience.

Second, in writing a simple sentence—"I remember I had a dog when I was five years old"—we are already at a distance from the experience because we are using the past tense. To get close to and remember more of the experience we use the present tense: "I am five years old and I have a dog." Step number two is to *use the present tense.*

Third, we *include our feelings.* "I have a dog named Spot. He is large and white and his tail wags all the time. I love to chase him all over the farm. When we stop, he licks my face. I like that." These observations are expressions of feeling and bring the reader closer to the experience.

Fourth, we *eliminate anything that sounds adult.* If we are sixteen going back to a time when we were five, we want to eliminate anything that a five-year-old would not say, though a sixteen-year-old might. We write in the present tense from the point of view of the age at which the event occurred. This brings us close to the experience.

Fifth, we get some *feedback* from others, learning beforehand how to give and receive nonjudgmental, noninvasive, constructive, and affirming feedback.

Sixth, we encourage *dialogue* to emerge. "I love to chase him all over the farm. 'C'mon, Spot run, run,' I say, running after him." This brings us even closer to the characters in the event.

Seventh, we *add inner thoughts* and feelings to the story.

Eighth, we find ways of bringing the reader into the story immediately through *action* or *dialogue* at the beginning of the story. "'Hurry up, Spot, get the stick.' I throw the stick and Spot runs after it. I am five years old and I have a dog named Spot. He is . . . ."

Ninth, we *identify the climax of the story* and *expand it*, bringing the reader into the experience even more.

Tenth, we add a life review postscript at the end of the story.

These steps apply to some degree to each of the levels of student writing. In succeeding chapters, we will look at each of these steps and see how they apply to children at each level of development.

The final outcome of these steps is the creation of a vivid personal experience in which standard fiction techniques—narrative, dialogue, and inner thoughts and feelings—are balanced with a believable point of view to bring the reader into the experience and keep him there.

Students who take the time to experience "writing from within" step-by-step will find improvement taking place in their writing skills. Clarity, improved mechanics and grammar, and a willingness to invest time in rewriting are a few of the benefits to come.

In this process, the writer learns how to balance the instructions of his or her inner critic with the urging of his or her creator in order to compose and review a story while profiting from the feedback of others to rewrite the story. This process will bring back to all of us, and particularly to children, our rightful heritage—the ability to tell a story well.

2

THE STAGES OF THE CHILD'S WRITING DEVELOPMENT

*"Every child is an artist. The problem is how
to remain an artist once he grows up."*
— *Pablo Picasso*

Imagine you are nine years old and your teacher asks you to write a story about your summer vacation. Your name is James (James the Jerk, according to your classmates) and you pick up your pencil. Just as you begin to think about your summer, a large gray ogre with bristly chin whiskers and sharp teeth seeps through the open window, floats over to your hunched up body and whispers in your ear, "You can't do that."

Let's suppose you don't hear the ogre's words, but instead you feel them in every part of your body. What happens? You get restless, you need to go to the bathroom, or you feel suddenly tired.

The ogre laughs at you, but you try anyway. "Last summer I went swimming. A lot. Every day. On Monday and Tuesday. One day when . . ." The ogre is laughing. You stop. "Better be careful," you think to yourself. "It was pretty funny when Johnny dove in the pool and lost his bathing suit and couldn't get out, but maybe I shouldn't tell . . ."

"Be careful," says the Ogre, "the teacher won't like it. She'll probably read it to the class and everyone will laugh and you will be so embarrassed, you'll . . . *pee in your pants.*" The ogre laughs hideously. Your hand goes numb; your head is heavy. You slump over.

The teacher comes up to you. "James, get to work," she says, picking up your paper.

"Teacher. I feel kinda . . ." you mumble.

She reads. She shakes her head. "No, this won't do. I want something good. Not days of the week. Get to work . . . or I'll read it to the class. In fact . . ." She does read it outloud. "I want something better than this from the rest of you," she shouts at the others in the class. The ogre laughs . . . and you learn to hate writing.

Sound familiar? For all too many adults, our writing attitudes and experiences have been shaped in this way: our ogre/critic undermines our efforts, creates doubt and frustration, and the teacher gives the ogre another voice. At other times, the critic's cautionary voice may be helpful in our writing, but for most of us the critic enters the picture far too early and blows us away.

As teachers, we can help our students identify, understand, and cope with their self-critics more effectively than in the past.

The Four Stages of Development

In this chapter we will look at the ways in which the creative spirit of childhood passes through four separate stages of development.

1. The Younger Child—(birth–10+)

2. The Middle Child—(12–14)

3. The Older Child—(14–16)

4. The Young Adult—(17–18)

By considering these stages of childhood in relation to the development of writing skills, we educators may be better prepared to help children deal with the obstacles to learning to write well that self-criticism poses. The older the child becomes (and the more rapidly she or he is moving toward analyzing and critiquing as habits of mind), the more the self-critic overwhelms creativity and expressiveness.

The "Writing from Within" process and the four stages

Although these age categories are narrow they correspond to dramatically different stages of writing development in children. Children will pass through each stage at different rates, but every child needs to go through each previous stage before going on. Each stage has rewards of its own.

This book shows parents and teachers how to use the nine-step "writing from within" life story writing technique to meet the needs of children in these four stages.

Stage one: Younger childhood

In this first stage (birth–10+), the child is brought into a world that is new and fresh. Nature is alive and teeming. People are large and

Make believe . . . is
a primary
spontaneous device
of childhood, a
magical device, by
which the world
can be transformed
from banality to
magic in a trice.
And its
inevitability in
childhood is one of
those universal
characteristics of
man that unite us in
one family.

— Joseph Campbell
*Masks of God:
Primitive Mythology*

powerful. Parents are the source of endless love, encouragement, and nurturing or pain, rejection, terror, powerful actions and feelings. When parents or other authority figures tell us to do something (or not to do something), we obey. This stage lasts from birth to about ten or eleven years of age.

During this stage, the child is encouraged to reflect back on vivid early memories (Step 1) and is encouraged to move from writing in the past tense to the present tense (Step 2). He or she is also encouraged to add feelings (Step 3), and finally, to write dialogue (Step 6). In this way, the child's stories will become more vivid and focused.

Stage two: Middle childhood

In the second stage (age 11–14), the child begins to hear and feel the critical voice within. The child does what he or she is told (or rebels) *even when the teller is not around*. At this stage the writer also begins to see that he or she has several legitimate writing voices; i.e., the personal writer as well as the analytical writer.

The child is encouraged to reflect back on early vivid memories (Step 1), to move from writing in the past tense to writing in the present tense (Step 2), to add feelings (Step 3), to learn to give elementary feedback (Step 4), to write from the child's point of view (Step 5), and to write dialogue (Step 6).

Stage three: Older childhood

In the third stage (age 15–16), the child is hearing his or her own critical voice strongly and is often in rebellion against all other critical voices, including those of teachers and parents. Brighter children will try outlandish writing effects that distance them even further from the authentic child's voice. The less confident will feel intimidated by everyone else's capabilities. The peer group is very powerful during this phase, often killing creativity if criticism is frequent or harsh.

The young person is taken through the above steps with more attention given to developing the abilities to communicate feelings (Step 3), to give feedback (Step 4), to write from his or her "inner child" (Step 5), to write more and better dialogue (Step 6), to develop a sense of form (Step 7), and to expand the climax (Step 8). The young writer will write focused, vivid accounts of experience, balancing observation, feeling, and effective storytelling.

Stage four: Young adulthood

In the fourth stage (age 17–19), the youth recognizes the distance he or she has come from childhood and can value both the innocence and creativity of the child within and the more adult, cautionary, objective voice within. More often than not, the adult values this cautionary voice as the one that will provide for survival in the phases coming up—leaving home, beginning a career, or going to college.

During this stage, the young person will become more comfortable with the techniques already discussed. The self-critic, of course, will be working with blast-furnace force to critique writing skills and life skills, anticipating the next phase of life: entry into the work force or into the ranks of college students. Conflict with authority is virtually a certainty during this phase, so a powerful need exists for writing techniques that allow the student to examine her or his grasp of the outer world of action while exploring the inner world of feelings—doubt, conflict, anxiety, outrage, embarrassment, confusion, and vulnerability, as well as obligation and responsibility. It is also the phase during which students can begin to assess the *meaning* of life's experiences with some depth by writing a postscript at the end of the story.

Whether age 10 or 17, students will develop from this process a stronger command of language and storytelling, as well as greater understanding and respect for the way they are handling their lives. They are also setting the stage for greater competence in other kinds of writing activities. (See Chapter 12, which addresses analytical writing.)

25

The
Stages
of the
Child's
Writing
Develop-
ment

STUDENT SAMPLES

Younger childhood: Natalie

I am going to begin by showing you the work of a seven-year-old who came to one of my senior citizen writing classes accompanying her grandmother. While the seniors in my class were reading their stories, Natalie wrote her earliest memories. That night she asked her grandmother where the family had come from. The following is her grandmother's answer as Natalie heard it.

child
book

From
Nathalie Chicha
271-6303
age 7½ yrs 7/6/6.

Grandpas Willies and Venture!

From stories her grandmother (me) told her. Doris Brandes

Written and drawn
by Nathalie Chicha

One of my favrit storries is cald Grandpas willies andventer. My grandma always tells me a story while I eat my dinner over the fire flames and it so heppend that grandpa willie whas my grandmas grandpa!

I think you would like the storie! Vont you?

So it started like this.
One day a band of salgers walked by the village of the jewish people. First the sallgers went to tabus house to warn him that the king was going to light a fire here.

Willbie was a helthy rish and handsome gent. He let the gews move to his propitorea by plane. They made and build new house. Then they put there houses were they wanted it.

Since they spend almost all their mony paying for the jewish village they went on wagon. They searched for a year untill they saw bosten.

Californya

Texes

Star

yend

Bosten

They moved to a very nice house in bosten. Every body helped bringing the boxes in.

As days passed it seemed that there were more things to do. One afternoon there was something strange out side. Mother saw it first. Then she cald the rest of the family. They look like Indians! said mother.

Finelly they Chuckir saw clearly. Mom I said janeo
their bowls! Well I don't know
everthing, said mother. Every body
laghed ensep mother she felt guity
of herself

The next day willie was
going for a walk. On the way
he bumped into an Indian
chief. What's wrong? willie asked. The
chief said: my people kicked me
out of my village. Would you like
dinner at
my house?
said willie
Yes said the
chief. Meet me
at 6:00 Brooke
Street drive
toninght. Oki
okl (willie thrmile!)

Willie told the family about the
Ind'ian chief. When the Indian
came mother setted the tabble then
she bronté out the food. It was
Hotdogs. Every body had just one
oranje because they were expesiv. Mothers
droped. She didn't pick it up because
she was afrian of the Indian.
Billy picked it up and ate it en-
front of his
mom.

You poisen me! You poised me!
when the Indian ate the
musterd thats what he said!
You pisen me! You poisen me!

The next week or so willie checked his pocket he had $40 left. He had an idia. The family went to a farm to buy a hen and a roster. Billy got to pick the best roster and susun picked the best hen.

Willie sold the hen and the roster to an Indian. The Indian gave them land and some money.

When they got home Billy asked his big brother Tim how Indians eat.

Tim took a book and looked up page 112. I says here that Indians boil the chicken. Then when it's done they pull of one fether at a time. Then they eat it.

But that's almost the same way we do it! said billy. I know. said Tim. Then he put the book away. Finilly their new bosten house became Home.

In twenty years I will
have children like you susun
always told her mom and she
did. Three girls and one boy.
I was the oldest girl.
And willie became grandpa willie.
Mother became grand mother.
Then Susun became a Mother.
Beth became an ant and Billy
and Tim
became
uclns!

Then my grand mother the
oldest girl of susun gave
birth to four girls and
one of the girls. gave birth
to me!

Then I ask If
it's the end and she
says yes!

30

This story illustrates the natural innocence and expressiveness of the child. We can see there is also an innocence to the way she plays fast and loose with facts. Research into the way children "see" at this age (see *Drawing With Children* by Mona Brooks) tells us that younger children see the world in a "flat" way, without depth, perspective, or a sense of time, although they can create a clear narrative sequence.

Expecting the child to write analytically at this point is no more relevant than asking Mondrian, Matisse, or Cezanne to paint with the perspectives of Leonardo, Raphael, or Michaelangelo. In fact the way the younger child sees is very much akin to the way modern artists who paint on the surface of the canvas see. Modernists such as Paul Klee, Andre Breton, and Joan Miro make every effort to enter this wonderful world that Natalie inhabits.

31

The
Stages
of the
Child's
Writing
Develop-
ment

Middle childhood: Lorena

Middle childhood is a period of transition. The middle child no longer sees the world in the innocent way the younger child does, but neither does she or he see with the eyes of the adult. There is a "critic" creeping into the child's work, in the form of an adult-sounding voice that is not his or her own.

The following story is by a 12-year-old girl writing at this stage of development. Later we will look at her work after she has been reintroduced to her child's voice—to her native ability to write from within.

First Memory
by Lorena Salazar
7th grade

I was about 6½ years old. I was in the first grade. It was time for my group to take its spelling test. We all go to the mat in the front of the room and the teacher instructs us to lie down and open our notebooks. I take a little paper from inside and check to see if anyone is watching. No one is so I slip it under the mat.

The test begins I know how to spell the first three words then on the fourth word I get stuck checking to see if anyone is watching

I lift the mat and check how to spell the word correctly. For the rest of the test I hide my scrap paper when we finish we give our notebook to the teacher an on my way to my desk I throw away the paper.

There are a number of things here that mark Lorena's work as adult-like, although most of us would take it for granted that this adultness is the correct way to write: the elements unfold in a coherent, logical way, and the writer uses the past tense to keep us at arm's length.

Now let's look at the work of Lorena after she has been reintroduced to her "inner child's voice," the voice on which she can build in order to create her own authentic writer's voice in the future.

First Memory
(second draft)
by Lorena Salazar

I am 6½ years old. I am in school and it is my group's turn to take the spelling test. The teacher calls out, "Group two, get your pencils and notebook and come to the mat." "Oh, boy," I say quietly, and slowly get my things and go to the mat.

"Spread out on the mat facing away from the middle," says the teacher. I do as I am told and when I am sure no one is looking I slip a piece of paper with the words written on it under the mat.

For the first part of the test I know how to spell all the words. Then the teacher says, "Spell second." I go over the word in my head.

"I don't know," I say to myself. After I check to see if anyone is watching, I carefully lift the mat and check on how to spell the word.

For the rest of the test I need to look at the paper.

"Turn in your notebooks and go back to your seat," says the teacher. I wait 'til the other kids begin to get up then I get the paper and hide it in my hand. I give the teacher my notebook and I go to my seat. I throw away the paper.

Notice how alive this version of her story sounds. She writes the story in the present tense and uses dialogue to make Lorena sound more like a real person—a 6-year-old, the genuine article—than she did in the first draft.

In the chapters to come, you will learn how Lorena came to make these changes. No longer does she sound like an almost-adult. She sounds like an expressive, interesting child because of the simplicity of words and the direct voice of the first-person point of view.

Now we will look at the work of a student in the early years of high school. In this stage the work is increasingly adult sounding; in fact, brighter students may sound more and more adult and far from the voice of the "authentic child" because they are trying to be more sophisticated and are beginning to read and copy the work of sophisticated adult writers. Here is Sonia O.'s story.

33

The
Stages
of the
Child's
Writing
Develop-
ment

Vivid Memory
by Sonia O.
10th grade

I was about 8 or 9 years old the first time my moma and my dad had goted into a fight which ended up as a divorce. I remember it was a bright, sunny day about 4 or 5 afternoon, I was watching t.v. babysitting my 1 year old sister, when I saw my mother closing her bedroom door and she started arguing with my dad, I didn't pay any of much attention at it, because I knew that maybe was some kind of momy's and daddy's argument. Afterwards, like an hour after I herd my mom screaming and yelling horrible things, they were throwing things to each other, and all of a sudden I herd a gun shot. I ran to the room I hit the door trying to open it, I screamed outloud "stop it, please stop it." My mom went out of the room and took my hand, grab my little sister and we left the house. That was the last time I saw my dad, none of them were hurt but that was the end of their marriage.

This story was written by a young tenth grader whose first language is not English. For example, the absence of a subject (" . . . I knew that maybe (it) was some kind . . . ") is common among those whose first language is Spanish. Likewise, there are numerous spelling, tense, usage, and punctuation errors common to those who do not know English well.

Nevertheless, there is a sophistication here common to those who are in the process of losing that immediacy of "childhood as a state of mind." For example, in her first sentence, she telegraphs to the end of the story: " . . . goted into a fight which ended in a divorce." Other examples are also there: narrative without much dialogue, distance from the event, an absence of feelings, and the use of the past tense.

Now let's turn to her revision and see what her story sounds like after she has learned how to recover her "childhood as a state of mind" with a teacher who encourages her to write in the present tense starting with "I am ___ years old and I am . . ." while adding feelings and dialogue.

Vivid Memory
(2nd draft)
by Sonia Ortiz

I am 8 years old, my mom and my dad are getting into a fight.

It is a bright sunny day, 4 o'clock afternoon. I am watching television and taking care of my one year old sister. My momther is closing her bedroom door, so I won't hear them screaming, telling each other ugly things that make me cry and scared. I'm trying not to pay any attention to it because is some kind of argument which I can not get into it. They have been fighting for more than one hour already, and mom is yelling and breaking everything in the room. I think my mother is asking him to leave her alone, but dady won't do it, because I herd him saying, "no, won't leave you alone, never." I call mom and I yell, "Stop it!" She walks out of the room, she get my hand and grabs my sister and we walk out of the house. I'm scared she won't talk to my dad again. (There is a divorce.)

In this version of the story, Sonia has recovered that innocent child inside herself. She is much more in the moment than in her first draft, and so are we as her readers. There is more of a sense of what the fight is about ("No, I won't leave you alone"), and it is much more believable because it is revealed through the dialogue. Likewise, in the second version her father's leaving is expressed, not as fact ("that was the last time I saw my dad"), but as a fear ("I'm scared she won't talk to my father again"). In fact, there is quite a bit of feeling described here (" . . . telling each other things that make me cry and scared").

Even the grammatical problems have diminished in subtle ways: " . . . had goted into a fight" has become " . . . are getting into a fight." Also, " . . . I didn't pay any of much attention at it . . . " has become "I'm trying not to pay any attention to it . . . " which is not only grammatically correct but is a fine observation of behavior under pressure. Despite the fact that there were no comments from the teacher regarding mechanics, the student has cleaned up many of the technical problems on her own.

Most important of all, it is clear that there is a developing awareness of relationships not possible in a younger child whose world is more self-centered. It is an awareness enhanced by maintaining contact with childhood as a state of mind—with the freshness and newness of life, of pain, of confusion, and of feelings of loss.

35

The
Stages
of the
Child's
Writing
Develop-
ment

Young Adulthood

During this stage the student will have developed a higher quality of self-examination. Once the student has broken through the tendency toward self-criticism, self-doubt, and creating distance between herself or himself and the event, an ability to balance the outer world of events and actions with a sense of the inner world of thought and feeling develops.

For a fine example of this kind of story please turn to the selection section and read Liz Kelly's *Tank Top*. The story is rich with examples of Liz's inner thoughts and feelings, balanced with the voices of people in the outer world who make her life more or less miserable.

Adulthood

The final phase—adulthood—is described in my book *Writing From Within* and, therefore, will not be discussed in this book. Examples are provided, however, in Part Three by writers in their middle and later years who have recovered their "childhood as a state of mind" voices and are in the process of reviewing their childhood experiences from the point of view of this child within.

▲ ▲ ▲

The stories from the first four stages of the child's writing development are the kinds of stories that can be taught in any classroom anywhere. Students love to experience their power to tell a story well. Teachers find their students are highly focused when they do this kind of work, and the students feel enriched as they progress, able to bring to the classroom their most intimate concern—their well-being and survival.

3

GETTING READY TO WRITE

"Children have more need of models than of critics"
— *Joseph Joubert Pensees*

Let us suppose you have a student named Sarah, a ten-year-old, in your classroom. Every time you give a writing assignment to your students, Sarah has to go to the bathroom. You allow her to go but when she gets back she draws hopscotch figures on her paper. Although Sarah may not realize it, she is confronting her fear of writing.

How can you help young writers overcome this terrible obstacle? First of all, you need to recognize fear when it pops up in different ways so that you can blunt its effectiveness. You also need to create an atmosphere in which the child feels it is safe to write, where good feelings, appreciation, and insight abound and there is little, if any, negativity and criticism.

These are the two concerns with which we shall deal in this chapter. If we help young people write well and then *affirm* that their effort has resulted in something good, we will go a long way toward removing the fear of writing.

One part of writing well is to pick an interesting subject. However, the more important part is to develop techniques and skills that make the most ordinary subject interesting. A helpful way of working on these skills is to divide them according to their use in the three phases of writing.

Although I will most often be addressing you as the teacher and guide to your students and children, please take the process to heart and also do all of the writing exercises yourself. The best way of learning to teach "writing from within" is for you to know, to do, and to enjoy the process before you teach it. In order to appreciate the child within your students or children, it is important that you are familiar with and honor the childhood state of mind in yourself. You will find that the assignments yield fascinating results for you, and for your students or children.

Discussing the Fear of Writing

With children over twelve, it helps to discuss "fear of writing." If your children are younger, you may wish to skip to the section "Write Without Stopping."

Begin by asking your middle and older students, "How do you feel about writing? Does it scare you? Do you feel fearful when you are asked to write?" If they answer yes, ask . . . "What are you afraid of?"

Their answers may include some of the following:

▲ fear of being unable to write well and being criticized by friends, parents, relatives, or teachers

▲ fear of being unable to finish or of getting off the track

▲ fear I might say too much and embarrass myself or someone else

▲ fear I just don't have what it takes to write well

Some or many of your students may say, "No, I have no fear of writing," although you may sense they are simply afraid to say they are afraid. Perhaps they cannot yet identify that fear. You may wish to ask the following questions as a way of helping them get in touch with these fears.

1. Do you go back and cross out parts of what you have written before you have finished your draft?

2. Do you find yourself getting bored or find your mind wandering in the middle of a writing assignment?

3. Do you find yourself wanting to do something else rather than doing a writing assignment?

Assure them that it is natural to be afraid of writing and that identifying that fear will help them understand what they are up against. How to deal with fear comes next.

You may wonder, at what age should children be asked about their fears? Children seem to become self-conscious and concerned about what others think around the sixth or seventh grade. It may happen earlier or later, of course, but around that time their written work reflects fearful concerns. They begin to be able to talk about their fears around this time as well, so the answer is "around thirteen."

Handling the fear of writing has two parts to it: first, understanding the nature of the *creator vs. critic* conflict; second, develop-

The first step toward playing is feeling personal freedom. Before we can play (experience) we must be free to do so. It is necessary to become part of the world around us and make it real by touching it, seeing it, feeling it, tasting it, and smelling it —direct contact with the environment is what we seek. It must be investigated, questioned, accepted, or rejected. The personal freedom to do so leads us to experiencing and thus to self-awareness (self-identity) and self-expression. The hunger for self-identity and self-expression, while basic to all of us, is also necessary for the theatre expression.

— Viola Spolin
Improvisation for the Theatre

ing an environment in which our "creator" is able to receive feedback from others (including parents and teachers) while feeling safe from them as "critics."

The Creator/Critic Conflict

Your students may say, "I don't really have any fear and I don't think I have much of a critic." That's wonderful, but let's give them a little test in order to find out.

Ask your student's the following question: "If you've been given a writing task and have written about a paragraph, are you inclined to stop at this point and go over what you've written or do you go on?"

If they reply that their tendency is to stop and go over the paragraph until it is "perfect," explain, ". . . You have a strong critic within and you will need to find ways to help calm that critic."

With younger children, simply encourage them to keep writing their stories without stopping.

Many children do stop and go over their work. They need to be encouraged to write to the end without stopping. Their work does not have to be perfect the first time. The best of our modern authors all say, "Just get through that first draft."

Research into the way the brain operates suggests there are two sides to the brain, left and right. Much of our fear of writing comes from the way these two sides work together.

We might term the right brain "the creator," for apparently it allows us to do creative things, such as make connections, create ideas, imagine situations, and see pictures of events. The left side analyzes things, puts them into categories, recalls words, and performs its learning functions in a step-by-step manner.

The analytical left brain has a little attic which houses the critic. It is the voice in us that says, "Watch out! You can't do that! You'll fail, so don't even try. You know you're no good at that!" And perhaps you would be right if you said that the critic sounds a lot like parents: "If I've told you once, I've told you a thousand times, you may not do (something you really want to do) until you have carried out the garbage, cleaned out your room, done the dishes, gotten good grades, etc."

The critic becomes a problem for us when we want to create something out of nothing, such as a story or a painting, because the right brain is very tender and sensitive to criticism. If our left-sided, tough-minded, parent-critic brain says, "Forget it! You can't do it," our right-sided, tender-minded creator says, "Fine! Okay! I'm going back to sleep. Talk to me again in a few weeks."

Right Brain

Left Brain

How do we counteract the critic? We calm the critic. We stroke the critic. When he or she comes out, we become aware of the presence but we do not fight. We want to avoid a confrontational stance with the critic ("What do you mean I can't do it! I can so!!"). To the critic, that is merely a call to arms. On the other hand, a flexible stance something like: "You'll be surprised what I can do," or "I've been doing pretty well, so I think I'll keep on creating, even if it seems kind of hard," will deflect the critic's thrusts and keep our creative juices flowing. Enjoy and be amused by the critic, but don't try to duel. The critic is actually valuable at a later stage when he or she is calmer and able to look at your work objectively. Then the critic can suggest ways to change and edit it.

We human beings have an almost infinite ability to censor ourselves. Fear not only keeps us from writing; it inhibits us from letting the world see our work when it is done. We tend to be very hard on ourselves as writers. In fact, some very good work may be lost because of our self-criticism, fears, and inhibitions.

Once we understand how our left-brain critic works, we can help our children work on their life stories by diffusing some fears and identifying the pressure of the critic.

If used properly, the critic can be a friend. Too often we give so much power to our critic that he or she dynamites our creator. We need to soften our criticism of ourselves and of our children and learn when and where the critic is friend, not foe.

As a parent or teacher you may be a bit of a critic yourself. If you take pride in what you do and how you do things, if you are a perfectionist to one degree or another, if you know you "ought" to be doing better at things than you are, your critic is strong and your children and students will feel it if your critic comes out at the wrong time.

Write Without Stopping

Encourage your students to *keep writing*. Once they have begun the story, keep going, even if it does not make much sense. Resist the urge to go back and make that first paragraph perfect. That urge is the critic speaking. Have them just plunge in without stopping. Don't worry about spelling and grammar. Just plunge on to the end.

Every artist has to warm up at the beginning of each "session" or "gig," as jazz musicians call it. Musicians do scales, actors do vocal and facial exercises, dancers stand at the bar and stretch. What can a writer do? Sharpen his pencil? Turn on her computer? No, warming up is an action, so for writers the warmup is writing. What comes out is not expected to be good. Unfortunately, most of us

I have discovered that you cannot start a book with intention, calculation. You start writing before you know what you want to write or what you are doing.

— E. L. Doctorow

expect the first thing out of the pen to be wonderful. This is true of children as well: if it is not wonderful, they feel stuck and won't go on. The best way of handling this situation is to encourage them just to begin and keep going. Later, after the good stuff has started to come and the child has gotten through to the end, he or she can go back over the beginning and cut out the "warm up" stuff. (How to "find the beginning" of the story is discussed in greater detail in Chapter 7.)

Write Large

Encourage students to write large and on every *other* line of a lined page. Skipping a line will enable them to make corrections more easily when the time comes to do so. They will also be able to read their work aloud easily and will feel more *free* in expressing themselves.

Revealing Private Experience

Some children will write about painful, intimate, or embarrassing experiences. These students need to be assured that they do not have to read aloud anything that is too personal to feel comfortable. If a student feels uncomfortable let him or her know you will look at the story privately, and ask the student to write another memory that can be shared more easily. If the student is simply very shy, encourage but don't force him to read aloud.

There is, however, another issue of an even more sensitive nature: what if a student reveals reportable offenses, including instances of child abuse. What do we as teachers do about this? In the Los Angeles Unified School District, teachers are instructed to let students know that any time a reportable offense comes to the teacher's attention, either verbally or in writing, the teacher is responsible by law to report it to the appropriate authority.

Therefore, let your students know that revealing a reportable offense in their stories, either as victim or perpetrator, will result in your reporting it, and, further, that the school counselor and possibly the responsible police agency, will take action. In some instances a student will write about such abuse anyway. In that case, telling his or her story is the student's way of seeking help in a sometimes desperate situation.

The life story writing we are encouraging with this method is *not* "doing therapy" in the classroom. It is not appropriate for us as teachers to use the method as a means of getting children to reveal the kinds of things appropriate for a counseling situation. This writing approach is intended and has been used to give students the opportunity to develop a command of language as a mode of communication. Within this developing command of language, it is appropriate for young people to see that having feelings, knowing what those feelings are, and expressing them on paper are entirely normal parts of ordinary life experience.

4

Recording Earliest Memories

"Maturity means reacquiring the seriousness one had as a child at play."
—Nietzsche

"Teacher, what is there to write about?" You've heard your students say it again and again. "I don't have anything to say." Inside themselves your students are saying, "My life is boring. Who'd want to know about me?" It is the same question most people ask when faced with the prospect of writing about themselves. The answer to the question is simple and not at all terrifying: focus on *the most vivid moments of life.*

The Three Phases of Writing

There are essentially three phases to writing a life story in an interesting, authentic way: *composing* it, *reviewing* it, and *rewriting* it. By following the specific steps that are part of each phase, you and your child or student can be assured that their work will be readable and enjoyable.

Writing about a vivid memory will take some skill, however, so it is best to start with one's earliest memory. Here they can learn some of the fundamental life story writing techniques before attempting longer, more complex memories.

Step One: Finding Your Earliest Memory

Their earliest memory is something children can see in their mind's eye, yet it is not too complex to describe. It will probably be a fragment of something or a piece of a picture. That is just fine. It does not have to be a story. Even a few lines will do. It's like playing "Twinkle, Twinkle, Little Star" when first learning to play the piano.

That little fragment, in fact, may turn out to be very interesting and revealing. One of my students in her seventies had been told all her life that she had hit her baby sister over the head with her bottle. What a traumatic memory to live with! But when she wrote about the actual incident, she recalled hitting the bottle on the side of the crib and breaking the bottle, which then hit her sister. Suddenly, she was relieved of a guilt that had haunted her all her life, and the relief was wonderful!

Begin by sharing an early memory of your own that is short and even fragmented. As with other writing assignments, modeling assists students in understanding the tasks and reassures them that they can do it, too.

Earliest memories are often dramatic—a birth or death in the family, leaving or arriving someplace special, a medical emergency. Sometimes, though, they can be as simple as remembering a shiny thing that hung over a crib. Have your students call up an early memory, no matter how simple it is. Just that. Nothing more.

Here are some topics that may trigger your students' earliest memories:

▲ My earliest happy experience

▲ My earliest sad or shocking experience

▲ My first experience with a birth in the family

▲ My first experience with a death in the family

▲ My first day in school or the first day I remember in school

▲ My first experience of being all alone without Mom or Dad

▲ My first experience in the hospital

▲ My first experience eating, playing, riding on a bus, etc.

If your students are having trouble identifying what memories were "early" and what came more recently, encourage them to write about something in the past even if it occurred only a week ago. Then take them backwards into an earlier time of their lives.

Okay, let's suppose your student has his or her earliest memory in mind. Now what?

Composing

Composing is the first phase of writing a life story. In a moment you will have your students do so by writing down their earliest memory without any further instruction.

Here is the first memory of a seventh grade remedial student at an inner-city Los Angeles junior high school. She has been given no instructions except that it needs to be her very earliest memory. This illustrates the kind of writing you may get at this point.

First Memory
Maria Sanchez
7th grade

When I was two years old my mom was teching me how to use the restroom sometimes when she teached me I would be scared because I thought I would fall in. When my mom was careing me up so I could sit on the toilet I would start to cry and I would say "No!" I don't want to sit down, I don't want to fall in. Then my mom would start telling me that nothing would happen but I refused to sit on the toilet then on tudesay my mom told me that I was going to do it again, but I refused to. My mom carried me up and took me straight to the restroom then my mome sat me down on the toilet but I said, "No, I don't want to go . I don't. I'll fall in. So then my mom made me sit down and then I wasn't scared any more. So then every 4 minutes I would tell my mom that I wanted to use the restroom because I wanted to sit on the toilet because I wasn't scared anymore.

We will follow up this story with a rewritten version in the *rewrite* section of this chapter and compare the two versions of the story.

As a teacher, you will want to instruct your students to give information such as "Where did it happen?" "How old were you?" "Why is it important?" Resist this urge. All of this will come out later. Right now we want put down on paper what they choose to put down. After all, this is a first draft.

When it is time for your students to begin writing, have volunteers tell their first (earliest) memory out loud (hopefully in the past tense). As soon as they have each had a turn, have them write the memory down on paper.

Reviewing

The next phase of writing a life story is for the student to review what he or she has done to see how the work comes across to a listener or reader.

If we review Maria's story we might observe that there are certain things the student does that keep us out of the picture. What does this statement, "out of the picture," mean? The objective of virtually every artist, no matter what the medium, is to draw us into the experience and keep us there. This is not so easy because most observers are skeptics on some level and so the artist, according to T. S. Eliot, must create "a willing suspension of disbelief." There are a number of things a writer can do to bridge this disbelief, or as I term it, the distance between ourselves and the experience.

What are some of the things Maria does to keep us at a distance from the experience? First of all, this moment is written in the past tense. This keeps us at arm's length. Second, there are few feelings described, and this also keeps us out of the picture. Finally, although there is dialogue (which certainly does bring us into the picture), it is buried in the story so we don't get a sense of its importance. These are all problems that can be easily and quickly corrected.

As an aid to the reviewing process, I strongly encourage you to have the students volunteer to read some of their stories aloud, after which you ask the listeners "Do you see the picture?" and "do you get the feelings of the writer?" (It is okay if they do not because you are going to show them techniques that will make the picture and the feelings clearer.) If the students are reluctant to read it themselves, you may do it for them. If the class is small, it is nice if all of the stories are read aloud, but *only* if students are willing. Reading stories aloud builds a strong sense of community and team spirit.

Rewriting

We are now at the final phase of putting together a first memoir: rewriting. The first phase, *composing*, involved freeing the writer to get the story down on paper without stopping; that is, without letting the critic grab hold and drag the writer back to redo that first paragraph. The second phase, *reviewing*, involved helping the student get some objective feedback about the work by having a friend or group listen and respond to it.

In this final phase, *rewriting*, students will learn how to make the story more vivid and substantially clearer to the reader while deepening its impact. Later, we will explore rewriting more thoroughly, but this first memoir needs only a bit of tinkering to make it work. It is, after all, just a moment from childhood and probably not even a complete story. Like a pianist learning to play the scales a note at a time, the present task is only to make this moment dramatic and believable. Before rewriting this first memoir, you can introduce the first steps in the life story writing process.

1. Write in the present tense, and in the first person.

2. Include your feelings ("I felt scared." "I felt happy.")

I alter a great deal, discard it and try again until I am satisfied. And then inside my head I begin to work it out, broadening it here, restricting it there, deepening it, heightening it . . .

— Ludwig van Beethoven

With younger children, simply instruct them to (1) change from the past tense to the present tense ("I was" to "I am"), (2) keep the voice of the writer in the first person singular ("I..."), and (3) add feelings. With middle and older children, explain the purpose of changing the tense to the present. Most will see how much more vivid the stories become when they are written in the present tense with feelings.

Step Two: Writing in the Present Tense

Students' very first efforts will probably be told in the *past tense*. But when your students go on to rewrite, have them do so in the *present tense*. Have them begin their stories with, "I am...".

Writing in the present tense gives readers a wonderful sense of being in the experience, rather than observing it. When we read a story written in the present tense, the events seem to be happening *now*, around us rather than far away as if recollected through a tunnel. A child knows only what is directly in front of his or her eyes. Therefore, we believe a story written from the child's point of view more easily if it is written in the present tense. We may lose some information, but we gain a great deal in dramatic impact and believability.

Writing in the present tense also has a benefit for us as writers: little details suddenly become clearer and more vivid in our memories. One additional advantage of writing in the present tense is that when we write this way, it somehow puts our critic to rest for a while. We get out of our reflective, all-knowing, critical adult selves and into our seeing, feeling, more innocent selves.

Writing in the present tense is not easy for some. Even young children have become accustomed to writing in the past tense for so long, it is hard for them to think of writing any other way.

Write in the first person

Another difficulty for some writers is allowing themselves to write in the first person. Often as students begin to write expository compositions, they are taught never to use "I," and after considerable drilling about this they have difficulty returning to the more natural narrative voice. If your students avoid "I," and tend to use "We," remind them: "You are at the center of your autobiography. You may report what others are doing, but you are the person through whose eyes and ears we, the readers, experience the event. You are important. It is okay to say 'I'." They will quickly get used to this welcome change.

Step Three: Including Feelings

As students begin to write their own stories, they may carefully observe what is happening without including their feelings in that moment. Encourage them to do so. Even if the students say they don't remember, encourage them to write what they imagine they must have felt. Often the writing itself brings back the feelings.

Resist the urge to make changes

The older the child, the greater is the urge to make big changes right away, even before he or she finishes this first review process. The urge to be critical is strong at this point. "It can't be any good, I'd better change it," some of your students will say. Urge them to resist that temptation. What students need most at this point is some feedback about the quality and effectiveness of what they have written from others who know how to give supportive feedback.

With younger children, you will have to provide most of the feedback. Simply help them confirm how much clearer the picture is between the story told in the past tense and the story told in the present with feelings added. Middle and older children can be introduced to the process of giving and receiving feedback.

Have your students rewrite their stories now, reminding them to write in the present tense and in the first person and to add their feelings to the experience. If your students are middle or older students, introduce them to the next step of the life story writing process for a second rewrite.

Step Four: Writing from the Child's Point of View

As we get older another problem arises: we stop sounding like children when we write about being children. We become more and more removed from the experience, sometimes walling ourselves off from the feelings of those early years. In "writing from within" we reverse this trend and get back to sounding like the children we were at any given moment in our lives.

Learning to write from the child's point of view is a very important part in the "writing from within" process. Most often this skill is developed in rewriting the story. Writing in the present tense is the first step toward doing this. The next step is seeing, then writing, the moment from the point of view of the child the writer once was. If the writer was in a crib, the reader might expect to see a bit of the crib sticking up at the foot of the bed where her or his parents might be staring down at the writer. Encourage your students to create a clear and truthful picture of what they see: the place where the event is occurring, the sounds and smells, and the atmosphere of the scene. However, if a student does not remember, it is okay. The students' awareness of these details will develop later as they get feedback from readers. They will learn what to look for in the past by understanding what the reader needs to know. Seeing the world through the eyes of a child, when the world was new and fresh, makes fascinating reading.

Some of you—teachers and parents of older children, perhaps—may be asking, "How in the world can I (or my high-school-aged children) write as a child would when I'm not a child? Shouldn't I just have them write as an older person looking back?" Though a teenager may not be able to write exactly as a child would, he or she can avoid certain writing patterns that mark the passages as those of an adult. The student is, after all, trying to recapture the world as seen through a child's eyes, not an adult's eyes. Have the student avoid using vocabulary, diction, and phrasing that a child could not possibly use. For example, consider the following passage:

> There were times, I suppose, when it seemed as if one would never be permitted to mature at a pace which was reasonable for my age. No, I was forced, albeit in a kindly fashion, to repeat ad nauseam the chores and duties attendant upon childhood: taking out the garbage, playing sports, minding my manners and obeying the strictures of my parents.

No one reading this passage would suppose for a moment that a child had written it, because children don't talk or write that way. Let us look at specific parts of this passage to see what is unchildlike about it.

Vocabulary and phrasing: "permitted to mature, reasonable for my age, ad nauseam, attendant upon" are all phrases no child, other than one attending college at a remarkably early age, would ever use.

Qualifications: Statements that are qualified or modified are rarely used by children. "I suppose" is a qualification, as is "albeit in a kindly fashion."

The Objective Voice: "One" is the objective voice and is virtually never used by children.

Lists: Cataloging chores, etc., in this manner is an adult way of organizing. Children may do it, but they are less orderly and logical.

Now, let us look at the passage after rewriting it in a way that may not be childlike but at least is not obviously adult.

From the time I was six or seven until I was eleven, my dad insisted that I take out the garbage every Thursday. What a chore that was! It seemed as if he'd never give me any real responsibility, just chores. But I remember one time when he . . .

Here you have a voice that could be adult or child. The passage is simple, straightforward, and visual. The narrator's voice and point of view do not intrude on the action or the progress of the story. Let's take a final look at the garbage incident rewritten in the present tense:

I am twelve years old. Dad makes me take out garbage every day. Gross! Everyday for six years. "When do I get a chance to do something important?" I wonder.

Suddenly, the story is more intimate, more vivid, more personal. This is the direction we shall pursue for our future stories.

Now let's look again at Maria Sanchez's first memory after her teacher talked to her and her class about using the present tense, starting with "I am . . . ," adding dialogue, and getting rid of anything that might sound adult.

First Memory
(Second Draft)
by Maria Sanchez

I am two years old and here I am in the restroom with my mom learning how to use the toilet. My mom is picking me up and sitting me down on the toilet. I'm really scared because I think I'm going to fall in.

"No, I don't want to sit down, I don't want to fall in!" I scream. My mom starts telling me nothing will happen. But I refuse to sit on the toilet. (Now,) it is Tuesday my Mom is telling me that I'm going to do it again. I refuse. My mom is carrying me up and taking me to the restroom. She is sitting me down on the toilet.

"No! No! No!" I keep on saying, "I'll fall in!

My mom sits me down and I ain't scared anymore. So every four minutes I tell my mom that I want to use the restroom because I'm not scared anymore.

With a few simple instructions from her teacher, Maria has found a vivid way of expressing herself. Her story creates a picture filled with feeling, gets off to a strong start right away, and keeps us in the moment all the way through.

It is time for your students to do another rewrite of their stories. Have them check to make certain they have written in the present tense, in the first person, and with feelings added. Have them take out anything that would mark the story as sounding older than the age at which it happened.

When your students have finished their earliest memories, you will see they have done what every writer does: compose, review, and rewrite. These are the same three steps they will follow with every story. As your students write their earliest memories, they will begin to find even earlier incidents and experiences coming to mind. The actual process of putting pen to paper seems to call up memories. Have your students write these as soon as they become vivid and significant.

In subsequent stories we will continue to write from the child's point of view, although as we begin to write our more recent stories, we naturally know more of past and present and can set the stage more fully.

Please see Florence M's story "Leaving the Plantation" (page 167) as an example of a powerful memory seen from a child's point of view.

NOTE: As students get older, they may well ask, "Why do we keep writing from the child's point of view like this. After all, we are not children any longer and our stories are not about ourselves as children." Have them continue to write from the point of view of the age at which the event happened using the same "writing from within" process they have been using. That way, they will keep the "childhood as a state of mind" experience alive within them. Moreover, you (and eventually they) will see an authentic writer's voice emerging, one stripped of all the adultisms (pretense, complexity, pseudo-intellectuality, distance) which so often mar the writing of many of us as we grow into adults.

Your students, particularly those of high-school age, may frown on the simple vigor of this kind of writing, yet it is this writing voice that will lead them to the clear, honest, insightful, self-reflective, and searching writing of which they are all capable.

Student Assignments

This chapter introduced you and your students to life story writing. Here is a summary of the steps used in writing the first assignment, "My Earliest Memory." Have students:

1. Go back as far as you can and find your earliest memory.

2. Tell it aloud in a group.

3. Write it down.

4. Read it aloud and then get some feedback.

5. Rewrite it, changing the verbs to the present tense, making sure the moment is written in the first person, and adding your feelings. Read it aloud.

6. Compare the differences between the two versions.

7. Older students: Take out any adult-sounding words or phrases.

You and your students have just written your first memory. Bravo! Keep Going!

5

LEARNING TO GIVE
SUPPORTIVE FEEDBACK TO OTHERS

*"'The grown-ups' ... advise(d) me to lay aside my drawings ... and
devote myself to geography, history, grammar ... at six, I gave up ... a
magnificent career as a painter. I had been disheartened."*
—Antoine de Saint Exupéry's narrator, The Little Prince

Paul Klee
wandered at will
from the heavy
world of the flesh
into the dancing,
whispering,
floating secret
world
of ... machines that
twitter, ... of a
baleful cat gripping
a bird image
between hypnotic
eyes ... (he) saw
the invisible, heard
the sound of
silence ... listened
to mute laughter,
and he felt the
movement of
growing things.

— Sarah Newmeyer
Enjoying Modern Art

Many of us who are teachers are actually fearful of writing. I, for
example, could do academic writing with ease throughout my years
in school. I also wanted to write creatively, but after one or two pages
into the story I would stop and go back. I'd try to make it better.
Soon the urge to write had passed and I would go play basketball or
pick up my saxophone. I was firmly in the grasp of my own
self-critic and I didn't know it.

Think back to your childhood. Did you have a critic advising
you not to try certain creative things? "You'll make a fool of yourself." "People will see you for what you really are." Yes, that voice.

Where do these critical comments come from? Usually our
parents and teachers and sometimes our peers and siblings. Sad to
say, it is too often a teacher in school whose harsh criticism stings us
into silencing our own creativity.

If our goal is to write, receiving thoughtless feedback can be
very damaging. When I was at UCLA attending film school, I wrote
a piece I was excited about for one writing class. In class, the
students seemed to find fault with every aspect of it so later that day
I tore it up. The following week I returned to class and the others
gathered around me, "So, how's that great story coming along?" they
asked. I told them I'd thrown it away. They were shocked, "We only
wanted it to be better," they said.

It is possible, however, to form groups within classrooms that
have entirely different dynamics. If the energies are positive and
supportive, then the writer is free to make mistakes, to open up
without fear, and to feel that the risks he or she is taking are
understood and applauded by the others in the group. In this way

the writer does not feel it necessary to defend his or her work and can, instead, focus on understanding how others are receiving it. Thus, the act of writing, as well as the act of giving and receiving feedback, leads to enhanced self-esteem, to better communication, and to feeling both closer to others and able to work with them as well.

Step Five: Creating Feedback

It is important for everyone who writes to get some feedback about what she or he has written. It is rather scary to ask for reactions, and it is especially scary if you are a child. Children's peers need guidance in how to give feedback, but once guided, their feedback can be a wonderful aid to the writer's effort to create.

Create a comfortable environment for writing

In order to write effectively, each writer needs to be in a comfortable place without interruptions. Have your students do the following:

1. Find a place where others will not disturb you. Perhaps you will need to go to a library, a senior citizen's center, or any place where the energy is quiet and where there are as few distractions as possible. Make sure there is enough light so you will not strain your eyes.

2. Find a comfortable time of day to let your mind wander. Most writers prefer the early morning or late at night. Each of us has body rhythms that are more apt to be creative at certain times. I myself write most effectively from about 7:00 A.M. to 12:00 noon.

3. Make sure you have several reliable pens or pencils with you so you will not have to interrupt yourself in the middle of your writing.

4. Allow your mind to drift. If you find yourself becoming sleepy as you are writing, go ahead and fall asleep. It is your mind solving creative problems in its own way. Just be sure that your mind is directed toward the writing concerns when you become sleepy and give yourself plenty of time to wake up and continue working on the assignment. After you awaken, you may see the experience you are writing about a bit differently.

Forming a group and giving feedback

Working with a group of friends or acquaintances, either in school or out of school, is very helpful. Reading memoirs aloud to a group will show students whether or not their stories are coming across well.

Ask those who are listening to the story to give the writer feedback about two things:

1. Can you (the listener) *see* the story clearly in your mind?

2. Do you (the listener) get the writer's *feelings* as you listen to the story?

Usually, if the story has an impact, the listeners may say that it reminded them of a time in their own lives when a similar thing happened. This is a very good sign.

Tips on helping children listen and give effective feedback

Listening to the stories other writers are telling can help develop insights into our own work. The first rule in reviewing others' work is to proceed with caution. Our biggest problem as listeners is that we want to be right and righteous. We want to be able to make the smartest comment, and we want to say nothing that will make us look stupid.

If we say too much, we will sound critical and may discourage the writer with our negativity. If we say too little, such as "I liked it," or "It was very nice," we give the writer no hint about how or where to improve the work, or we may give a false sense of effectiveness.

At what age can children be introduced to giving feedback? Experience tells me that some children as young as nine years old can give good feedback, at least about feelings. For the most part, children in the seventh and eighth grades can begin to give good feedback. They can certainly be asked if the picture was complete and what emotions they felt when listening to the story.

Teaching supportive feedback

We have all encountered criticism from different people during our lives. We probably remember how stung we felt when teachers, parents, and even friends criticized us when we were doing the best we could. Such criticism was especially painful when we were doing something artistic: writing, painting, drawing, or playing a musical instrument. Often, we simply stopped doing these artistic things.

Gradually, we internalized this criticism and developed our own inner critic.

Now we are in a position to help our students handle that painful feeling. With younger children, we want them to experience creating and writing in a nonthreatening way. With older children who already have a built-in critic, we want to try to retrain their critic.

If we don't do this, our students may not go on writing after the first bit of harsh criticism they receive when they share their work with others. Training one's inner critic is no small or easy task. It can be accomplished, however, with patience, discipline, and a positive outlook. In Chapter 5 we will explore teaching feedback more fully. There I will outline a process by which the wild, undisciplined, even destructive critic within can be converted to a purposeful, disciplined, insightful one.

Early childhood feedback

With children in the early childhood stage of writing development, the most effective way of developing their positive critical voice is to have writers read the first and second version of each assignment. Most children, even quite young ones, will notice the differences.

Even younger children may also profit from some of the techniques of giving feedback that follow, particularly feedback about "seeing the picture" and "feeling the feelings of the writer."

Each child might be encouraged to keep a checklist of things to look for when giving feedback, such as:

1. Can you see it?

2. How does it make you feel? Happy, sad, some other feeling?

3. Does it feel finished?

Middle and later childhood feedback: NJNICA

A group, or even one person, can help the middle and later childhood writer get the kind of feedback she or he needs by making and sticking to the following agreement among participants, including teachers and parents.

Feedback to each writer after she or he shares a story will be *nonjudgmental, noninvasive, corrective, and affirming* (NJNICA, for short). Each person giving feedback agrees to avoid any statement that sounds judgmental or invasive, no matter how innocently he or she intends it. During the early sessions of any group one person may be appointed to be on the lookout for such judgmental and invasive statements.

Typical *judgmental* statements sound like this:

"You should/ could/ought to have . . ."

"If I were you, I would . . ."

"That (story, thought, paragraph, etc.) was too (sentimental, clever, abrupt, silly, slow, confusing, boring, etc.) . . ."

Typical *invasive* questions sound like this:

"Why did/didn't you . . . ?"

"Why were you . . . ?"

"You sound like you were trying . . ."

"You often/always . . ."

Any one of these statements can discourage a writer. Instead, ask members of your group to try the following nonjudgmental *corrective* statements:

"I would like to see/feel/know/be able to follow . . ."

"I had trouble seeing the picture."

"I had difficulty following the action."

"I needed to feel the character's feelings."

"I found my attention wandering."

"I needed/wanted to hear the characters talk to each other more."

And for older, more sophisticated writers:

"I had difficult finding/following the spine."

"I didn't know what the central question of the story was."

"The key question was answered before I had a chance to get involved or excited about it."

Or, these nonjudgmental *affirming* statements:

"I saw the picture clearly."

"I was right there with you the whole time."

"I knew what each character (or the narrator) was feeling from one moment to the next."

Affirming

"The dialogue drew me in and helped me get to know each character."

"The balance of narrative, dialogue, and inner thoughts and feelings held my interest."

These are important considerations. A potential writer can listen all day to these positive comments. He or she can listen for only a few moments to invasive or judgmental statements before beginning to defend himself or herself, shutting off creativity, and stopping writing.

You may find that your child's support system is only one person—yourself. One person is enough if his or her feedback is noninvasive, nonjudgmental, corrective, and affirming, though having even one additional person giving feedback really helps. For example, if yours is a family setting, and you are a mother bringing your child along in "writing from within," try to get a father, sibling, or grandparent involved, but be sure you train them in NJNICA feedback first.

The great advantages of working in a group or with a friend (or better still, with two friends) is that the writer can stop being the critic and simply create. Each person can then be a responsible critic for the other writers when they read their stories. A very workable number in large classes is groups of three: one to read a story, one to give feedback to the writer, and one to keep the person giving feedback on track.

If you are a teacher of middle and later childhood students, use the phrase, "Okay, let's get some comments now," after the student finishes reading his or her story aloud. Let the students say as much of what needs to be said as possible. Make your own comments after the children finish theirs.

The exercises below will help students develop nonjudgmental, noninvasive, corrective, and affirming feedback. They may be tried alone or in a group *before* your students write their stories or *during* the time they are writing their stories. It will feel safer for them to begin learning the feedback process with these stories rather than having their own stories as subjects.

1. Review the first draft of "Willem," which follows. Allow members of the class at least one class session for the story. Appoint one person to roleplay the writer and a few to give feedback. The writer may defend what has been written any time he or she feels the feedback is hostile, judgmental, invasive, or superficial. When the critique of his or her work is over, have him or her tell the others what it felt like, who was providing NJNICA feedback and who was not.

2. Encourage each student to give feedback and describe his or her responses to the story aloud. Tell students to focus attention on how they responded to the story, rather than on how the story is written (i.e., "I needed more detail," "I found my attention wandering," rather than "It's too long," "It's too confusing."). You play the writer. Tell your students that if you begin to defend yourself, it is a clue that the feedback is judgmental, invasive, or superficial. Encourage the group to find a NJNICA comment that will make the same point.

Remind your students that by giving NJNICA feedback that focuses on reactions to the story, the listeners leave the writer room to make choices about what to change and what not to change. Have each person in the group defend or absorb feedback for five minutes. Continue until each person in the group has had a chance to roleplay the writer. The comments may be repetitive, but the purpose of the task is to (1) have them experience being a writer under the gun, and (2) enable them to begin to change their mode of giving feedback from critical, judgmental, or superficial to NJNICA.

3. Address the following issues through discussion:

    ▲   Is the point of view childlike or adult?

    ▲   Is the story written in the present or as a recollection?

    ▲   Is the level of language that of a child or an adult?

    ▲   Is the situation believable?

    ▲   Are there enough details to make the picture clear?

    ▲   Are the writer's feelings clearly expressed?

Have students try to rewrite the story, taking into consideration their own feedback.

Finally have the students compare their versions of the story with the way the author actually rewrote it. You may wish, once again, to appoint one of the students to defend or explain or simply compare and contrast the differences between their rewrites and the author's. Assure them that there is no one right way to do these stories. They are attending to the task of creating feedback and promoting lively discussions.

Willem
by Jade
Age 65

I have no recollection of the first years of my life. Looking way back into my early childhood, I come up with this little picture, a picture that has surfaced every once in a while whenever I am thinking of the old days. I must have been three or four. There was a big sprawling backyard. A tall hedge concealed the main house, some distance away. The house was quiet; my mother must be resting. It was siesta time, the time after lunch when the shimmering tropical heat made people drowsy. It was also Sunday, the drone of my father's machines was not there. My father must also be resting. My father had a house-industry at that time. He bought up spices such as pepper, nutmeg, cloves, cinnamon, etc. from the farmers overseas on the other island, then he ground and bottled them in a special building on the grounds.

To assist him he asked Willem to come over from his hometown on a far island to work as his foreman. Willem also lived with us in an outhouse.

I liked Willem, because he always spent time with us, whenever there was a chance. That afternoon was no exception. He showed my brother and me some magic tricks and then he said, "Kids, I am going to show you how strong I am!" He asked Joni, another workman, to go fetch the bicycle. Then he lay down on the grass and Joni was told to drive over his chest.

I was greatly impressed when Willem stood up unhurt. Then he said, "And now the van will drive over me." Again he lay down on the thick grass and supposedly the car drove over him.

I was in awe that nothing happened to Willem. This was where I got befuddled. I am sure I had not told my mother then and there, because she would have taken some action regarding Willem's way of entertaining us and she would have remembered the incident. As it was, when years later I talked about it, mother said, "Nonsense, he must have tricked you." But I still wonder, did it really happen or was it just my imagination?

▲ ▲ ▲

Willem
(Second Draft)
by Jade

I am sitting in the grass. The grass is a cool green and very thick and soft; I sink in it. I like to sit there. The sun is very bright, but the hedge behind me makes a shade. My brother is there, too. He is bigger than I. Papa and Mama are not there. I know they are in the house a little far away behind the hedge. But Willem is there. He is very big, almost as big as Papa. I like him. He always has something nice for me and my brother. What will he do today? He is lying in the grass. There is also Joni. I do not know him too well, but he does not matter. Willem is there! Willem is saying: "Anak mau lihat Willem digiling sepeda?"

"Kids, want to see the bike run over me?" Joni already goes to fetch the bicycle.

There he comes straight at Willem lying in the grass. Then the bicycle is already on the other side of Willem and Willem is standing up and laughing. He laughs at us kids. And then, with a laugh in his eye, he tells us, Papa's big truck will now run over his chest. Again he lies down in the thick grass, the car comes and it is over him; only his head sticks out; he is laughing at us. I hide my head. I am afraid and I grab my brother's hand. But I still look. Willem is already up again. Willem can do anything!!! Years later when I talked about it, mother said, "Nonsense, he must have tricked you." But I still wonder, did it really happen?

This rewrite of "Willem" is a much simpler story than the first version, isn't it? This version gives us the feeling of being *in* the event rather than watching it from a distance. In fact, we feel as if the event is happening to us, as if we are the child watching the truck go over Willem, wondering how such an awesome thing can happen.

As a teacher, you may be saying, "This is all well and good, but I have thirty kids in my class. How do I handle this?" I have often been faced with large numbers of students taking my workshops and classes. What works very well is to have the students break up into groups of three. Have one person read a story, one person give feedback, and the third person keep the second person on track in terms of giving only nonjudgmental, noninvasive feedback. As the teacher, you can go around from group to group and listen to the feedback and to the tracking of the feedback.

Summary

This chapter has addressed the importance of providing—and training others to provide—nonjudgmental, noninvasive, corrective, and affirming feedback (NJNICA) that will truly assist students as they review and rewrite.

Compare the first and second versions of a volunteer's writing, beginning with the *earliest memory*. Ask student(s):

"Can you see what's going on better than in the first version?"

"Can you feel the feelings more? What are the feelings?"

Clearly, we should never compare a student's work to another student's. We also should not compare a student's later work to earlier work except to say that it is more *effective*, because everything a child writes is valuable and valid.

Student Assignments

Feedback for early childhood writers

1. Can you see a picture in your mind?

2. Can you feel the feelings of the characters?

3. Does it feel finished?

Feedback for middle and later childhood writers

1. Note the "distancing" effect of techniques in "Willem" (first draft). Compare and contrast the first and second versions.

2. Apply techniques discussed in "Early Childhood Feedback" to students' earliest memory.

3. Apply NJNICA feedback to earliest vivid memory assignments and all subsequent memories that are read aloud.

As the teacher or parent intending to teach these techniques, the very best way for you to make them your own is to form your own feedback group and write some of your own stories.

6

FINDING THE MOST
VIVID EARLY MEMORIES

"The truly great artist has the eyes of a child and the vision of a sage."
— Pablo Casals

"My life looks like an unending piece of sausage," lamented Paul, one of my senior citizen students some years ago. In fact, many of my students have expressed this feeling. "What's so interesting about my life?" asks Kathy, a nine-year-old in one of the parent-child workshops I have conducted. Well, what we have to do is find ways of tying off tasty little "links" that can be bitten off and consumed with ease. The best and most tantalizing way is to tie off the most vivid memories and feast on those. If a student can do this, his or her life will suddenly begin to look much less dull and boring.

Writing: The Most Vivid Memory

Let's start by having your students go back into the past in search of their *most vivid* early memories, memories that stand out more than any other early memories. It may be an escape from a threatening situation when they were very young; it may be a special celebration; the death of a dear friend or relative; a time in their lives when they left or came to live in a special place; or going to school for the first time.

This early vivid memory should not be confused with one's earliest memory, which may simply be a tiny fragment of a recollection like some archaeological relic from an ancient time. No, we are looking for an early memory that has power and strength. It should occur some time between birth and 12 years of age.

Composing

Begin by reminding students to follow the writing tips discussed in the previous chapter as they write about an early vivid memory:

▲ Write in the present tense.

▲ Include your feelings.

▲ Eliminate anything that does not sound as if a child could write it (at the age of which you are writing).

Here are a number of topics that may bring to mind some of the vivid moments of your students' lives:

▲ Most vivid memory of parents

▲ Most embarrassing moment in school

▲ First adventure

▲ First time being really afraid

▲ First success in school

▲ Most vivid recollection of Grandpa/Grandma

▲ First kiss

▲ First time getting into trouble

▲ Happiest time in school

▲ Best friend in school

NOTE: remind students that if the memory is uncomfortable or painful, they should feel free to go on to another memory.

▲ ▲ ▲

Here is a vivid memory recalled by a young boy writing in a remedial class in an inner-city Los Angeles seventh grade classroom.

The Train
by Fernando Reyna
Age 13

The first time I jumped on a train when it was moving, The train was about 10 blockes away from where we were at. The train was moving about 7 or 8 mph. When it got to where we were at we got anxious and nervous because it was my first time doing this. My friend got on the train first then me. but my other friend couldn't get on but he did when he reached

I was walking in the street or sitting on a train and overheard a remark dropped from the lips of some man or woman. Out of a thousand such remarks, heard almost every day, (are) the seeds of stories.

— Sherwood Anderson

the street. When I got on the train whells almost cut my leg of because when I got on my foot was on the latter but then it slipped and I almost would've got my leg chopped off if it wasn't for my other leg being on the latter. I was able to pull myself up and save my leg.

We will look at a rewrite of this memory in the *rewriting* section.

Having your students write their most vivid memory will be a bit of a stretch for some students. The following are two tips that will make the process easier.

Have your students write down everything they saw and experienced at once. Insist they not stop, even if the pieces are disconnected. Insist they not stop—not for anything.

Reviewing

Encourage students to keep a checklist of steps to apply when reviewing their own and others' stories.

Checklist

1. Can I "see" the story clearly?

2. Is my story told in the present tense? Did I write in the first person?

3. Have I included my feelings and thoughts?

4. Did I write believably from a child's point of view (leaving out adult words or changing them so they are believable)?

For those of you teaching younger children, I suggest you tailor this section, including the checklist, to your own needs. In particular, I suggest you not worry about Step 4, writing believably from the child's point of view. I have found that even young children *love* to write dialogue and do it very well. As an exercise, have them pair up, talk for one minute to each other, then each write down the dialogue and read it to each other.

Then have your students give one another NJNICA feedback. One point to bear in mind is this: the feedback is *for* the writer. She or he does not have to follow any advice or feedback. It is there to use if she or he so desires.

Now that students have completed their first drafts, we are going to add another ingredient.

Step Six: Creating Dialogue

Perhaps you have heard this comment about some of the students' stories from their classmates or friends: "It was a good story, the picture was clear, and I got your feelings, but somehow I still didn't feel close to what was happening." Another technique that will help bring the reader or listener closer to the action is *dialogue.*

Suggest to students that they begin by trying to remember what their characters actually said way back when. If they cannot quite remember what was said, have them write down what they think might have been said. Suggest to them that something inside of them will say, "Yes, that's close," or "No, that doesn't feel right at all." Improvising dialogue this way will carry them closer to what actually was said, provided they *write,* not just *think,* the words they are seeking. In general, have them try to keep their dialogue to a sentence or two each time a character speaks.

Introduce your students to the use of quotation marks: in order for the reader to know that he or she is reading what the characters say to one another, the writer inserts quotation marks (" . . . ") around the spoken material.

Mother said to come here now, becomes: Mother said, "Come here now."

When your students write dialogue, have them put the "he/she said," (or replied, etc.) *after* the dialogue: *"Come home,"* Mother said; or in the *middle* of the dialogue, after the first phrase if possible: *"Come home right now,"* Mother said, *"And don't go out again before dark."* Avoid placing the "he said/she said" at the beginning of the phrase or sentence: Mother said, "Come home." There is more surprise for us if we hear the dialogue for a moment before we learn who said it. But we need to know who is speaking shortly after that person begins to speak.

This is also the place for your students to learn the correct format for dialogue. Explain to them that each new person speaking gets a new paragraph, and model the following example for them.

"Get out of here," Mother says to me. "Get out right now!"

"But Momma," I answer. "I wasn't doing . . . ."

"Don't you sass me, young lady!" Mother's eyes are very hot and angry and I am afraid.

Knowing and using this form allows the child to begin to see people as clear and distinct from one another. This is important as they move from the younger childhood stage of development on to the middle and older childhood stages of development.

The students are now ready to begin rewriting their stories. They have a number of techniques at their disposal and an understanding of what these techniques can do. They have the feedback of others to help them, and they understand how to analyze their first draft.

We tend to think of rewriting as taxing, boring, or even painful, but the results are almost always worth the effort. To have one's work go straight through to the mind and heart of the reader feels wonderful, as the students are no doubt finding out.

Here is Fernando's story *after* his teacher discussed the previous checklist points with his class and then had the students rewrite.

Train Ride
(2nd Draft)
by Fernando Reyna

"The train is coming!" my friend is yelling excitedly. The train is still pretty far away from where we are at. The train is moving at a running pace. I'm anxious because it's my first time doing this. First I will get on then my friend Sergio the my other friend. (Now) I'm running with the train with my hands on the ladder. I'm jumping on, my right leg is steady on the ladder but my left leg missed the ladder and I'm about to get my leg cut off by the wheel(s) of the train. Luckily, I am strong enough to pull myself up and save my leg.

Notice what an enormous difference there is in Fernando's writing with the story told in the present tense, with his feelings included, and with a bit of dialogue included. He is *in* the story the whole time and we are as well. The story becomes much more vivid when he uses phrases such as "the train is moving at a running pace" rather than "the train was moving about 7 or 8 mph."

▲ ▲ ▲

This concludes the work of the younger child in terms of learning new techniques. Many wonderful stories can now be written using the techniques learned so far. If the younger child shows great promise in this work, she or he should be encouraged to work on the following two steps for middle and older childhood.

Techniques for Middle and Older Children

The most important concern for us at this stage is that your students become accustomed to adding dialogue to their stories, either in the first draft or in the rewrites, so pay particular attention to this step as they rewrite.

Once they have given thought to various areas of improvement, have them read their stories over and make changes where it feels right to do so. Do not try to rewrite on a step-by-step basis. Have them give some thought to the following two concerns as they rewrite.

Form and structure: Focus

A vivid memory may in fact be a series of vivid memories, so each student needs to develop a sense of where the episode begins and ends and write only one episode at a time. This is called *focus*. Classically, such as in an Ibsen play, a play begins only after some important event has taken place: a death, a crime, etc. Encourage your students to begin their story as close to the *most vivid moment* of their experience as possible. What is important is to get the *reactions* of the major characters throughout the episode and to know when the incident or event ends. Focus is also related to finding the "spine," which we will discuss in a moment.

Focusing on what the episode is about, finding where it begins and ends, and writing using vivid details together make up what we call narration or storytelling.

Ultimately, the students will be seeking a balance between narration, dialogue, and their inner thoughts and feelings.

Form and structure: Finding the spine

Form gives one's work some definable shape, so that the readers or listeners may know where they are going and can enjoy where they have been. A story about a duck needs to be about a duck. A story about an uncle needs to be about an uncle. As a writer, this involves giving the reader little clues about what to look for, a coherent thread or even a running gag. Sometimes a mood or an atmosphere running through a story can also provide form. Stories can hang heavy with memory and emotion. This, too, is form.

Each story has its own emotional logic and concerns, and the line of that logic is the "spine." Anything else should be left aside, or saved for another story. Other concerns, issues, and people need to be addressed at a later time. Finding and keeping to the spine is closely related to structure. Since the mind can hold just so many things in it at one time, we have to limit the mind's attention to those things that are related to the spine.

Let's suppose, for example, the beginning of our first draft is about taking a trip from Russia to the United States, the middle is about finding a house to settle in so that Mom, who is sick, can feel better, and the end of the story is about Mom's death and how everyone felt.

From the ending we get a clue about the spine and the structure.

In fact, the middle—Mom's getting sick—is also a clue. The beginning needs to relate to the end, so the beginning of the story needs to be about Mom's health or well-being. The trip from Russia is clearly a separate story.

Writing Another Vivid Early Memory

Composing

At this point, let us begin another early vivid memory following all the steps we have learned so far.

Reviewing

Have your students use the checklist to reviewing their own stories and others' stories as well:

Checklist

- ▲ Can I "see" the story clearly? If not, what do I need to do to make it clear?

- ▲ Is my story told in the present tense? Did I write in the first person?

- ▲ Have I included my feelings?

- ▲ Did I write believably from a child's point of view, leaving out adult words or changing them to be believable?

- ▲ Did I include interesting dialogue?

Now, have your students give one another NJNICA feedback using the checklist.

Rewriting

We want to continue to add to our techniques and concerns, so we will now address two additional aspects of writing which we will introduce during the rewriting phase.

1. More about writing your feelings and inner thoughts

2. Creating transitions

Step Seven: Write About Inner Thoughts and Feelings

You may have noticed that some of the stories or incidents which your students write about really stir up emotions in you, while other stories, though they may be descriptive and have good dialogue, feel incomplete. Something is missing. What is missing is usually some level of feeling that needs to be in the story.

There are ways of getting more feeling into the student's writing, ways that will cause readers or listeners to remember a story and say, "Now that really stirred me up."

Each of us has what we might call an inner eye. When events occur that cause us to feel and reflect from a place deep within, that inner eye tracks these feeling and reflections. All writers can use this awareness to deepen stories.

Most of us have had the experience of talking to ourselves, sometimes muttering aloud, sometimes keeping it inside our minds. When we talk to ourselves aloud, it is called monologue. When we talk to ourselves inside our heads, it is called inner monologue. Inner monologue is a very effective device.

Creating a strong sense of our feelings is also very effective in our stories. As we learned earlier, we can draw the reader into the story in a very powerful way when we add our responses to any description of an event or dialogue. "As I listen, I feel the anger rise up inside me" or "I feel sad the whole way home."

We can also deepen the reader's experience of our feelings by recording the physical sensations in our body as we respond to events that produce emotion in us. "My stomach begins to cramp," "my eyes fill with tears," "my heart begins to race," "my legs ache."

As a teacher, you can help your students become much better writers and more aware human beings by encouraging them to add inner thoughts and feelings to their stories.

Here is an example of the use of these techniques from a writer who could be twelve or thirteen years old in the story.

A Vivid Memory
from Birth to Twelve

I walk in the kitchen, open the refrigerator door and take out the peanut butter jar. Mom is at the counter slicing cucumbers.

In theory few men
are as free as a
playwright. He can
bring the whole
world onto his
stage. But in fact
he is strangely
timid . . . there is
either the author
who explores his
inner experience in
depth and
darkness, or else
the author who
shuns these areas,
exploring the
outside
world—each thinks
his world is
complete.

— Peter Brook
The Empty Space

"Go to the store and get some bread," she says, in a cross voice. She doesn't look at me, just keeps slicing cucumbers.

"Oh, heck!" I think to myself. "I want to watch Batman on T.V. and finish my model airplane." I stop in the middle of the kitchen.

"Did you hear me?" she continues, banging the knife hard on the counter. I go into the dining room and slump onto a chair. "C'mon, get off your backside," she says. She comes into the dining room and sticks two dollars in my hand and goes back in the kitchen. I hate it when she bosses me around. She never lets me do what I want. "Go on!" she orders. "Now!"

I hate it when she does this, treats me like a little dog go here, go there, do this, do that. "Ahhh!" I say to myself, "Why can't some else do it?" Patty, my sister, always gets to do what she wants. Momma never asks her to do anything. My heart is pounding. I hear momma's voice in my ears. It's like a bell. "Go on. Go on. Go on . . ." I close my eyes for a moment and grit my teeth. My head starts to hurt. "What's wrong with you?" I ask myself. "Why don't you ever stick up for yourself? Huh?"

"Ok," I say. I start out the door. I feel so awful, so . . . kicked around.

Notice how the inner thoughts ("Oh, heck . . . I wanted to watch Batman"), inner monologue ("Why don't you ever stick up for yourself?"), inner feelings ("I hate it when she . . . treats me like a dog"), and sensory feelings ("my head hurts") all work together to create a strong sense of how the child is experiencing this moment.

You may be asking yourself, "At what age should I expect children to include these feelings and thoughts?" It is appropriate for kids of twelve or thirteen to begin expressing themselves this way. Even younger kids can begin to if they are skilled in the previous steps. Age is less a factor than whether the student feels comfortable with the process up to this point and can do the previous steps easily.

You may wish to demonstrate to your students what inner thoughts and feelings are without insisting that they add thoughts and feelings that they are not yet seeing or feeling. "Just add some inner thoughts and feelings where it feels right," you may say to them. Later, you can remind them to continue doing so in subsequent stories, demonstrating places where you would like to hear those inner thoughts and feelings expressed.

Transitions

Some of my students find that in their stories they need to move from one time period to another. In stories written in the past tense we might find expressions such as "later," "after that," or "soon after." Writing in the present tense generally requires a more specific time reference, such as, "Now it is three months later, and I am..." or, "The year passes quickly and I now find myself...." Generally, these are effective expressions that enable the student to get from one specific moment to another quite easily.

Editing and rewriting: Making a distinction

Now may be the time to talk to your students about editing and make the distinction between rewriting and editing clear to them. *Rewriting* alters the content and style of the stories to make them deeper, more meaningful, and clearer. *Editing* brings the grammar, usage, spelling, punctuation, and the like into conformity with generally accepted practice. Editing is a left-brain task that needs to be kept quite separate from the creative, right-brain rewriting task. Editing in this sense is a polishing task to be done at the end of the final rewrite and never between drafts.

Most students are quite terrified of rewriting, partly due to their confusion between editing and rewriting. They try to do both tasks at the same time and wind up doing neither well. If we can get them to rewrite when it is appropriate to rewrite and edit when it is appropriate to edit, perhaps we can diminish some of the fears and make the experience a little more positive.

As you will see in the chapter on teaching life writing, we strongly encourage you to bring the editing tasks to the student slowly, without placing much emphasis on them in any one assignment.

Student Assignments

1. Find your most vivid memory between birth and twelve years old.

2. Write it in the present tense and in the first person (I am ...).

3. Review it, get feedback, and get rid of anything that sounds adult.

4. Rewrite, creating additional dialogue. Make sure it has a strong spine.

5. When you have done this earliest vivid memory, do another.

6. Follow all the steps you have followed up to this point, reviewing and rewriting as needed. In your rewrite, add more inner thoughts and feelings.

7. When finished, edit for grammar, punctuation, and the like.

7

Revising and Revisioning

"I have rewritten—often several times—every word I have ever published. My pencils outlast their erasures."
— Vladimir Nabokov

By now, at least some of your students are having a wonderful time with the techniques they have been taught. They are continually at work on rewriting stories to make them more interesting and more readable. For these high achievers, there are three other techniques that will make their stories tighter and more effective:

1. Finding the beginning of the story

2. Expanding the climax

3. Adding a postscript

Step Eight: Finding the Beginning of Your Story—Dialogue and Action

Here are a few simple steps your students can follow in order to find the beginning of the story.

First, have them ask, "What is the most powerful moment of this vivid memory of mine? What is the moment I remember most clearly?" Then ask, "Can I start my story just before this vivid moment begins?" Usually, as writers, we give much more introductory information than the reader needs to know, which can be left out or rearranged.

After your students have finished a first draft, suggest they look over the story right away and *spot that first line of dialogue or action*. Often, the closer we get to the most vividly recalled moments in the story, the more dialogue we will naturally write. That first line of dialogue may be a clue to the beginning of the story and to the spine of the story as well.

Remind students not to worry about starting off their stories

If I started to write elaborately, or like someone introducing or presenting something, I found that I could cut that scrollwork or ornament out and throw it away and start with the first true simple declarative sentence I had written.

— Ernest Hemingway

73

with a perfect opening when they are writing their first drafts. Finding the beginning is strictly a rewriting task. All artists need to warm up. Musicians do scales, actors do vocal and facial exercises, dancers stretch. Writers have to warm up, too, and that is what the first few paragraphs of each draft are—a warm-up . . . until rewriting begins. The first line of dialogue or action is where we writers begin to hit our stride. By that time the writer is into the story and so are the readers.

There is another reason why finding that first line of action or dialogue is important, rather than beginning it with establishing atmosphere, as most stories do.

Who Am I?
by Isaac Bashevis Singer

I was born in the town of Radzymin, near Warshaw the capital of Poland, on July 14, 1904. My father Pinchos Menachem Singer, was a rabbi, a highly religious man. He had a red beard, long black side-locks and blue eyes . . . . Early in 1908, when I was three years old, my parents moved from Radzymin to Warshaw. . . . I was curious by nature. I observed grownups, their behavior. I listened attentively to their talk . . . . At an early age I started to think all kinds of thoughts: What would happen if a bird flew in the same direction forever? What would happen if a ladder were built from the earth to the sky. Our apartment at 10 Krochmalna Street had a balcony and I would stand on it for many hours and muse.

The difficulty with this opening is that we have no idea where it is going. The best way for us to know where we the readers are headed is if the opening line provokes a question—which is sure to happen if it begins with a line of action or dialogue.

Let's suppose that the author had written:

What would happen if a bird flew forever in the same direction? What would happen if a ladder is built from the earth to the sky?

We would conclude that the child is very bright and very curious, wouldn't we? We might wonder what will happen to this curious child, thereby anticipating other stories that tell us the answer. We might also wonder how he got to be so searching at such a young age, which would, in turn, set us up for the author's giving us some information of the kind he gives us in

I am five years old and these are the questions I ask as I play outside where I live in Warshaw, Poland.

Once we have asked ourselves these questions, the spine of the story has been established and we have been hooked by the questions that we, as readers, now want answered. So a good, strong beginning entails creating a strong, vivid opening that causes the reader to ask the right questions.

The first line of dialogue or action will usually get the reader to ask, "Who is saying/doing this? Why is he/she saying it? Where/when is it taking place? What's going to happen?" These are typical journalist's concerns (who, what, when, where, why, how) but as a writer you want to avoid giving answers to these questions until the reader asks the questions first.

Finding the beginning of your story:
Creating a backstory

When we use dialogue and/or action to begin a story, a number of questions arise in the minds of readers and listeners almost immediately: *What is going to happen? Who is doing what to whom? Why is it happening?* and *Where is it taking place?* A good story will address all of these questions soon after the curtain goes up, and it will answer most of them by the time the curtain descends. Creating a backstory or "setting the stage" answers the question: *what information does the reader need to know in order to understand what is happening at the beginning of the story?* Teachers of writing often instruct students to give this information to readers at the outset of the story. Also, as students write without instruction, they tend to provide this information right away almost as a matter of warming up to the story they want to tell. It is fine as part of the writing process that they do this; however, this "setting the stage" information is not what the reader needs first. As we discovered in the previous section, the reader needs, first, to be drawn into the story so she or he will want to know the answers to questions such as, who, when, where, what, why, and how.

Once the reader is involved, the writer can begin to provide this information, which in the film world is called the "backstory," the part of the story that took place before the story opens.

This vital information is best told to the reader in the second paragraph of the story rather than in the first. My rule of thumb is *never tell the reader anything until he wants to know that information.* So let's look at the earlier example from Isaac Bashevis Singer.

Who Am I?
by Isaac Bashevis Singer

I was born in the town of Radzymin, near Warshaw the capital of Poland, on July 14, 1904. My father, Pinchos Menachem Singer, was a rabbi, a highly religious man. He had a red beard, long black side-locks and blue eyes . . . . Early in 1908, when I was three years old, my parents moved from Radzymin to Warshaw . . . . I was curious by nature. I observed grownups, their behavior. I listened attentively to their talk . . . . At an early age I started to think all kinds of thoughts: What would happen if a bird flew in the same direction forever? What would happen if a ladder were built from the earth to the sky. Our apartment at 10 Krochmalna Street had a balcony and I would stand on it for many hours and muse.

The information in paragraphs 1 and 3 is all good backstory and becomes more interesting when we move, "What would happen if . . . sky" to the beginning. In this way we see that setting the stage or providing backstory to the reader is just a matter of rearranging our thoughts to make the story more interesting.

During my years as a writer and director in the film industry, I observed these same techniques at work in motion pictures. Early filmmakers, like writers of the nineteenth century, often gave the viewer an establishing shot—a wide shot encompassing a whole city or village—then brought us closer to particular dwellings or places, in a medium shot. Then they would create a more intimate bond with the characters in a series of close-ups. Take a look at *Covered Wagon* from 1923, which opens with a long procession of covered wagons stretching across the plain and then moves in to closer shots.

Modern filmmakers often reverse this process: first comes the tight shot to reveal a character's identity and feelings. Then the film widens to include a sense of what action is occurring and where it is taking place.

Students can easily borrow a page from the filmmaker's notebook to give the reader a quick glimpse into the emotions and identity of characters through dialogue, then to provide some backstory in the second paragraph. Make sure, however, that your students grasp the idea that writing backstory first is the most natural thing in the world for them to do; this "cinematic" way of beginning a story is a matter of rearranging paragraphs that the students have already written.

Here is another point you may wish to make with your students: if they are twelve and older and are writing stories about themselves when they were younger than ten years old, writing from a child's point of view, backstory or setting the stage might actually be hard to believe at the beginning of a story. The child's world is tiny and narrow, though fascinating. As young children, we see the world through a very small window. We know little of what others are doing. We know nothing of past and future. It is a very particular stage setting. As we mature, the window through which we see the world widens. We know more of past and present and of life beyond ourselves. At this point, we can provide more backstory, though we continue to set the stage in the second paragraph.

Remind students that setting the stage is not a matter of inspiration or great talent. They do not have go to into a creative trance in order to create a solidly visual picture. In fact, the beginning of the story can be lightly sketched at first and the details of time and place filled in later when the story is about to be completed. Encourage students not to bog themselves down in these details when first sitting down to tell or write a story.

Step Nine: Expand the Climax of Your Story

"I wanted to know more of what was happening at the climax of your story," a listener said to one student. I realized that several writers were getting that same kind of feedback, so I began suggesting that they expand the dramatic moment when everything comes to a head—that is, the climax of the story.

In films, for example, a dramatic moment of action or feeling can be captured in slow motion or repeated in slow motion from several angles. In one of the more memorable scenes from the movie *A Man and a Woman* by Claude LeLouche, the camera circles two lovers as they fall into each other's arms at the train station as if spinning a web around them and sealing them off from the world outside, slowing down everything so it seems these passionate moments exist outside of time.

Such cinematic techniques allow the reader/listener/viewer to understand and savor every moment of this wonderful experience. Similarly, successful baseball players describe the ball coming to the plate as large as a basketball and moving slowly—easy to hit. Everything slows down and the moment when bat strikes ball expands.

This is not to say that the writer is trying to slow down the action of the rest of the story. Rather, the final moment is expanded and illuminated for the reader. The other techniques we have learned—including more dialogue, more reactions from the minor characters, more of a sense of any changes taking place around the action has the effect of speeding up the action because the story becomes fuller and more complete.

In the following paragraph taken from "Tank Top" by Liz Kelly (see page 156 for the full text), the first draft ended with the line, "... turn and walk back." After getting some class feedback, Liz decided to make the final moment fuller by adding what happens next—her futile discussion with the school counselor. This is "expanding the moment."

Tank Top (excerpt)
by Liz Kelly
Age 18

"Liz, what's wrong?" Lori asks. "Nothing," I say as I turn and quickly walk away so they won't see me crying. I only take a few steps then I dry my eyes and turn and walk back. "Liz, there's something wrong," Lori says. She puts her arm around me and guides me into the counselor's office. Mr. Cothern, the counselor, gives me a knowing look. I've been here before. Lori sits me down in a chair and I put my face in my hands and cry. Lori leaves to go to class and Cothern and I go into discussion. I can't live with my father anymore," I tell Cothern. "I can't handle it." Cothern gives me a serious look. Well, as serious as his looks ever get. Mr. Cothern is a tall man that reminds me of a character out of a cartoon strip. His eyes are always laughing and I don't think he takes me seriously. "Cothern, I'm serious." I try to convince him. "Liz, your dad isn't going to move out, and if you stick around things are going to get better. You can work them out." "Fine," I say. I sit and listen a while longer then I go back to class. I know, only too well, that things are not going to change.

Step Ten: Add a Life Review Postscript at the End

During the course of developing this approach to writing I have found some students wanting to assess the meaning of the vivid moment to their lives, to update the reader on its significance or to add some vivid detail that may not have been possible in writing from the child's point of view.

I began suggesting that they add a "PS" at the end. To some of them it seemed artificial. However, a significant number began to see that by asking themselves, "What has this moment meant to me?" and "What did I learn from this moment?" the process of developing self-awareness moved ahead much more quickly.

There are certain phrases a writer can use to add such a postscript. "As I look back, I can see that ...." is one such phrase. "It is

_____ years later now and I can see that I was . . . ." is another. As the writer looks backward, it is appropriate for him or her to use the past tense to suggest the "reviewing" process.

At what ages do children begin this process of self awareness? Experience tells me that it develops gradually through each stage of the writing process. Most of us develop this kind of awareness of ourselves as we begin to separate from our parents, so as teachers we might expect this process to accelerate during our students' my-parents-are-my-problem or where-are-my-parents years.

An example of this kind is Liz's postscript to the story you have just read:

PS: Shortly after this in incident, which occurred when I was sixteen, I dropped out of school, left Wyoming and came to Southern California where I began working as a live-in housekeeper.

On my one morning-a-week off, I came to one of Bernard's life writing classes. It was a great help to release these feelings and begin to see more clearly what I had been through.

I'm twenty and living in Santa Cruz, CA. Over the past year or so I have been sharing the stories with my family. It has not only helped clarify my feelings but has helped other members of the family begin to express their feelings as well.

At long last the whole family is beginning to deal with my father's rage, and the alcoholism which has often unleashed it.

A Final Checklist

1. Can I "see" the story clearly?

2. Is my story told in the present tense? Did I write in the first person?

3. Have I included my feelings, including my inner thoughts?

4. Did I write believably from a child's point of view (leaving out adult words or changing them to be believable)?

5. Have I gotten some helpful feedback about my story before going on to rewrite it?

6. Have I created interesting, believable dialogue?

7. Did I include some inner thoughts and feelings?

8. Did I find a strong beginning to my story based on dialogue and action?

9. Is the climax of the story as full and rich as possible?

10. Do I need a PS at the end? If so, have I written one?

Summary

As we have seen, much of our best work emerges from the rewriting of our stories. Have your students look over their stories to see if they can be improved by improvising some dialogue, by finding and staying close to the story's spine, by finding the best possible beginning to these stories, by expanding the climax beyond a few sentences, and by adding a postscript where it is appropriate.

If your students take the time to follow these steps in rewriting, they will be surprised and pleased at how interesting and believable they will have made their stories and by how much they may have learned about themselves in the process.

Student Assignments

1. Find another early vivid memory, this one about a relationship of some kind, with people talking to one another.

2. Follow all the steps outlined in the previous chapters for composing and reviewing.

3. For the students' rewrite, look for the beginning of their stories. One clue is to have them look for the first line of dialogue or action. This may be the beginning of story. It is always effective to begin a story this way. The information between the opening line of the story and the first line of dialogue or action may be shortened and used as a second paragraph for "setting the stage."

4. Another effective way of finding the beginning is to identify the climax of the story and see if the story can begin much closer to the climax than it does now. See if the climax can be expanded with more dialogue and more inner thoughts and feelings.

5. Have students ask themselves, if appropriate, "What did I learn about myself?" from this incident. Have them add postscript notes to their stories, if necessary.

8

CREATING FAMILY STORIES

"Finding out who parents are and were, beyond their roles as mothers and fathers, is a family business that many . . . leave unfinished."
— *Margie Patlak*, LA Times

Bringing the Family Together

Years ago, a woman in her middle fifties came to one of my classes wanting to learn how to tell her family and friends what it was like to have polio. Long after she had finished those stories she was still writing, explaining that "my family enjoyed the stories of my child-hood so much that I just have to keep writing." For her children it was a chance to discover who Mom really was. Eventually she began telling the stories of other generations as well, and the members of her family responded by coming to visit her from all parts of the country.

This way of pursuing a family history allows family members to glimpse stories from the past and the relationships out of which these stories have come. It helps members feel proud of and close to those who have come before.

Up to this point in the book, our efforts have been directed toward helping students learn how to tell their own life stories. Now we can use these skills and techniques to help them record someone else's story. There are essentially two ways of doing this:

1. Have your students record an interview with the subject on audio- or videotape and transcribe the session onto paper. These are called *oral histories*. Methods of interviewing and questions to ask can be found in Appendix B.

2. Have your students write down their *experiences* of listening to parents, grandparents, or other family members telling stories of the past, while capturing the relationship that existed between the student and the storyteller at the time the story was told. We call these *family histories*.

81

Writing Family Stories

Many of us who set out to write life stories are primarily interested in writing about the struggles and history of our parents and grand-parents. Typically this kind of story is a simple narrative retelling of the past.

> My grandfather was born in the Ukraine. When he was 16 he was forced to serve in the Czar's army. After a year he escaped and made his way to America.

While reading this sort of narrative, we the readers find our-selves asking a number of questions: How did the narrator hear about his grandfather? Who told him the story? How do we know it is true? How did the people involved (the grandfather and the narrator) feel about these events?

Out of a need to answer these questions, a more authentic way of telling family histories is one in which the feelings of both the storyteller and the writer are evident while the story is unfolding.

"When writing this kind of family history," I tell my students, "let the reader know how you learned about the story. Were you sitting on Grandma's knee or taking a walk with Grandpa? Let the reader know what you remember Grandpa or Grandma doing or the feelings he or she reflected while telling you the story. That way we get both the story and your relationship to the storyteller. We will believe it and feel it more fully." John Strong's "How I Became a Rebel" is a good example of this kind of writing. Although it is not specifically a story told to John by someone in the family, it is the kind of story that would certainly be preserved in the family.

How I Became a Rebel
by John Strong
Age 69

My great grandfather served four years in the Union Army. As a courier, Corporal Dillen once delivered a top secret message to President Lincoln. He was with Sherman's army through Georgia and was severely wounded at the Battle of Chicamauga in Tennessee. My great-grandfather raised my mother, so many of his Civil War stories were handed down to me. Also, my great-uncle was lucky to survive the infa-mous Libby Prison, where he languished for a year. I had several other relatives in many battles, so I was a true-blue Union "veteran" at the age of eleven. Union veterans now in their nineties visit our school every Lincoln's birthday. Word goes around that this is to be the very last visit at our Clymer, Pennsylvania school because of their old age. They always speak to our assemblies about education, citizenship and good morals, but never about the battles of the war. I decide to do something about this on their last visit. "I think it would be alright," says Miss Brady, our teacher, consenting to my staying in at Recess and talking to one of the old soldiers. The one I select is more alert and more erect than the other six. His uniform fits his slim figure as though a tailor had made it. It has a blue satin-like sheen unlike the crumpled rough cloth of the blue uniforms of the others. He has a twinkle in his blue eyes and wears his forage cap at a rakish angle. He had been a first lieutenant in a Pennsylvania Regiment. "Mr. Hill," announces our teacher, "John loves history and would like to ask you some questions." "Certainly," replies Mr. Hill in young sounding voice that surprises me. "Mr. Hill, you soldiers always talk about dull things like that we should get a good education and never talk about the Civil War. Can you tell about some of the battles you were in?" I begin. "John, those battles were terrible," he replies seriously. "The history books tell all about the bravery and colorful aspects of the war; however, the bloodshed and suffering was awful. I saw my own brother killed before my very eyes! It is still a horrible memory." Then Mr. Hills changes the tone of his voice. "I will tell you something, John, that you, being interested in history, will never forget."

I lean forward as he begins. "After the war, My Cousin Ralph, a Union soldier also, and I were endeavoring to select a college to attend. Ralph wants the University of Pittsburgh, but I suggested another school. 'Why don't we enroll at Washington College in Lexington, Virginia?' I said. 'Why down in Rebel Country?' he replied, surprised. 'Because General Robert E. Lee is the President of the College,' I answered. 'He was a great General and an honorable man. The school he heads will be a good one.' 'You know, of course, the students will be all young rebels. Why, we would be the only Union soldiers in the whole school.' 'I don't like your choice at all, Jim,' protested Ralph. 'Besides, he was the commander of the Rebel army, the very ones we fought against for four years.' But I win out, so we enroll at Washington College. For two months we never saw General Lee, then one day, we were summoned to his office.

"He sat in a big chair behind a desk and told us to be seated. I studied General Lee's face as we sat in silence for a few moments. He was more handsome then the photographs you see in history books. Of course he had gray hair and beard, but it was his tan face and large brown eyes that attracted my attention. His dark eyes, almost black, went from my face to Ralph's, as he spoke. 'How do you like it here at the college? Are the courses satisfactory? Do you think the instructors are well-qualified?'

"To his three successive questions, I answered with an emphatic, 'Yes, sir. We are well satisfied, General Lee!'

"My quick affirmative answer seemed to please the General. Then after a minute or two, he explained. 'Actually, I called you two men here out of curiosity. Why would you men, former Lieutenants in the Union Army, select this small school when you have so many fine universities in your native Pennsylvania? Furthermore, almost all the students here were in the late Confederate Army and that includes me.'"

"General Lee waited patiently for my reply. I stood up as did Ralph.

"'General Lee, we knew that you were the best general in the late war and that you were a gentleman. Any college you headed would be of the best, and we have found it just that!' My eloquent little speech even surprised me, the speaker.

"General Lee arose from his chair and walked toward us, never leaving his eyes from our faces. He was well-built with broad shoulders and about six feet tall, as were Ralph and I. General Lee now stood before us. With a trace of a smile, he extended his hand to me, then to Ralph, with a firm clasp. 'Gentlemen, you will never know how much those words mean to me,' he asserted with what I thought were tears in his eyes.'" Now Mr. Hill looks up and says, "Now John, isn't that a better story, and it is true, than one about the bloody battle of Gettysburg?" "Thank you, Mr. Hill," I say. "Thank you very much. But General Lee was the Commander of the very army you fought against. Why did you admire him so much, Mr. Hill?" "You see John," explains Mr. Hill, "General Lee did everything in his power to try to get everyone to forget the war. In processions at the college, he would purposely march out of step. He never published his memoirs like many other generals. He refused to lend his name for an insurance company in England, where he was greatly admired. He never gave interviews about his battles. General Lee owned no slaves. He resigned from the U.S. Army when his state of Virginia seceded in 1860.

"Almost every southern officer in the U.S. Army did the same thing. It would be like Pennsylvania seceding. Wouldn't you have gone with your native state, John?" asks Mr. Hill. "Just before the surrender, some of his officers wanted General Lee to break up his army into guerrilla bands so as to hold out until the Federal government got tired of the war. General Lee wouldn't see to that. At the surrender, General Lee had 30,000 men. General Grant had 130,000. That's the type of General he was—undermanned, lacking in food, and equipment, yet holding out. For a young fellow, those remarks may be hard for you to think about, but try to remember this tale."

▲ ▲ ▲

I have remembered those remarks for about fifty years now. General Lee and the Confederates, Stonewall Jackson and Jeb Stuart have fascinated me more than the Union Generals, Grant and Sheridan. I suppose my grandfather Dillen and other Union relatives were spinning in their graves because of my preference. I guess they can thank Mr. Hill for this.

John, a onetime Pennsylvania coal miner and World War II army officer, wrote this story years before many of the principles of the "writing from within" approach were developed. Here is the way he *might* have written it now.

How I Became a Rebel
(imagined revision)
by John Strong

I am 11 years old and in elementary school in Clymer, Pennsylvania. The year is 1924. One day the teacher tells us, "class, we have a special treat today. We have two visitors . . . who fought in the war between the states. They are here to tell you about it." A few moments later they walk in. Two of them. They are old. With beards. Today is veteran's day so they wear their uniforms, blue tunics with blue pants. One has the bars of a lieutenant on his shoulders.

They walk slowly and sit down. I am eager to talk to them. On both my father and mother's side of the family, I have relatives who fought in the Grand Army of the Republic the union army. At the first chance I get, I raise my hand. "Sir," I say, "could you tell us about being in the war. What it was like?" The old man's eyes twinkle. "I suppose you want me to tell you about the bloody battles, don't you." I nod. He shakes his head. "I won't do that. War is hell. Absolute hell. But I will tell you a story about the war," he continues. He leans back in his chair. His eyes get a far away look. "The war was over. The bloodiest damn thing you ever saw. My cousin Ralph and I decided we wanted to go to college together. We were lieutenants in the GAR, the union army and we wanted to stick together.

"So we chose Washington University in Virginia." The old man smiles down at me. His eyes are soft. "We enrolled in classes there. General Lee was the president of the university but we didn't see him much. Occasionally a parade in the mornings.

"But he marched out of step, on purpose, to make himself ordinary, nothing special. But we admired him nonetheless. Almost all the other men there had fought for the south. After all, Gen. Lee had been their commander. They'd 'ove followerd him anywhere.

"One day we got a note from the office of the president of the college asking us to stop by. When we arrived the General was waiting for us.

"He was a soft-spoken man. A little shy. But powerful. I almost saluted him. He came right to the point. 'Gentlemen, I suppose it has not escaped your attention that most of the boys at this here school were once under my command in the late war...' 'Yes, sir,' I said, eager to say something. 'Well, then, since you are the only two fellows from the union army enrolled down here, officers too, I wonder...if you might tell me...why? Why did you come here?

"I looked at my cousin and he looked at me. Finally I spoke up. 'General, sir, my cousin and me, we figured that you were the best general of any of 'em, north or south. Wherever you went that was the place for us.'"

The old soldier stops for a moment. He takes a glass of water and drinks. Finally he goes on. "The General stood and looked at us then nodded. There was a faint smile on his face. 'You'll never know how much that means to me,' he replied, shaking hands with us both. We left...." The classroom is as quiet as an empty church. The old soldier looks around the room at each of us. "Think about that boys."

Notice that in the story John speaks in the present tense, as if Clymer, 1924, were the present; but when the old soldier recollects the past, he speaks in the past tense. This is because the old soldier's recollection of 1865 was the past, even in 1924.

Notice also that John's soldier speaks directly to us, as well as to him. The result is that we experience the story through John's eyes. It is important for us as readers or listeners to know through whose eyes we are experiencing events at every turn in the story. This knowledge creates belief in the story. It also increases our interest because writer and teller have a relationship to share with us in addition to the subject matter of the story itself.

A hundred years ago we would not have thought to ask "From whose point of view are we seeing the story and is it to be believed?" Until the middle of the nineteenth century, writers like Poe, Dana, Scott, Thackeray, Hardy, Melville and many others told their stories from a god-like or omniscient narrative point of view, and we accepted this point of view as truthful. But in the writings of Stephen Crane, Henry James, and James Joyce, and in the dramas of Pirandello, readers became more aware of the person through whose eyes the story was being experienced and seen and the particular bias that point of view could introduce.

As contemporary readers, we no longer take for granted the truth of a story unless we know something about who is telling it. By recording the relationship of the storyteller to the writer of the story, we get a more authentic and believable view of the family history that is being told.

Wonderful stories of one's family can be written by people of all ages. The story by Natalie Chicha (page 26) is a good model for this kind of storytelling from a younger child's point of view. Middle and older childhood stories might look more like John Strong's story.

Student Assignments

For younger childhood writers

1. Have your students ask their grandparents (or any older person) to tell stories from their childhoods.

2. Have the students record the story on a tape cassette.

3. Encourage your students to illustrate the stories with pictures, as Natalie did.

For middle childhood writers

1. Have your students' grandparents (or any older person) tell a story of their childhood. Be sure the child writes down how he or she responds to the story.

2. Encourage students to do some research about some subject the older person touches upon in the story.

3. Teach children about footnoting and bibliographies so additional information can be added to the end of the stories.

For older childhood writers

1. Have your students' grandparents (or any older person) tell a story of their childhood. Encourage the writer to provide a sense of himself or herself in the story in addition to the story that was told.

2. Encourage writers to do some research about a subject the older person touches upon in the story.

3. Teach children about footnoting and bibliographies so additional information can be added at the end of the stories.

9

WRITING FROM TWO POINTS OF VIEW

"Writing from within" can also provide members of the family with an opportunity to convey to one another their various and divergent points of view. By divergent points of view I mean conveying differing experiences, but not necessarily differing attitudes and opinions. In this way, children and parents can compare their different "takes" on a shared experience with the real possibility of sharing hurts and confusions without blame. Children can begin to see that their parents differ in their perceptions of situations and that sometimes the only real truth is each person's perception of it.

The following examples demonstrate what kinds of vivid and powerful writing can flow from differing experiences within the family.

On a Clear Day
by Jeri
Age 50

The year is 1989 and I am in San Francisco visiting my twenty-one-year-old son, Jim. He has been living in San Francisco for the past two years. I've looked forward to this trip for a long time, and feel a grand thrill both for being with Jim and for being here in this glorious city after 30 years. We've made a loose agenda of what we'll do in my three days. "I really want to go to City Lights Bookstore," I tell him. "Do you know where that is?"

"Sure no problem, you'll love it there," he says. "Can we ride a cable car?" I ask. "I've never ridden one before." "I think it can be arranged," he says and smiles at me like I'm the child now. We laugh. "So what do you say we eat lunch."

We find a restaurant with a view of the bay and order lunch. Over lunch, our conversation drifts to the family that Jim hasn't seen for awhile, his cousins and aunts. "What's Pat been up to?" he asks, referring to his cousin who is eight years older. I think about his cousin Pat for a moment and the secret I carry about him, then I reply, "Oh, he's still doing well; he and Glenn are still landscaping for the rich and famous." I grow quiet and thoughtful for a moment and then I continue gingerly, "You do know that Glenn is gay." He nods. Although we've never spoken of this before, I don't expect him to be surprised to hear that news about Glenn. What I am really concerned about is how he will take the rest of the news that sooner or later, he's going to have to know.

Outwardly Jim's cousin gives no clues. I sure never gave it any thought. I feel the burden of the secret and go on avoiding it.

As gently as I can, I say, "Jim, Glenn has AIDS." I watch it register on his face. "Shit," he says, and I see the look of anguish come over his face. I reach across the table to him. "I know, I know," I say, trying to comfort him. Somehow the burden of the real secret becomes too much and the words, " . . . Pat is gay . . ." tumble out of my mouth.

The words seem to hang in the air. I decide to leave it at that. He doesn't need to know the rest, not yet, I think. After all, the rest of the family doesn't know yet. He drinks the last drop of his coffee and says, "Let's get out of here. I'm finished, how about you?" Outside, the sun is glinting on the water of San Francisco bay as we walk slowly around the wharf. Jim has his arm draped loosely on my shoulder and we are both quiet for what seems like a long time. As we walk, I am acutely aware of how much he is the image of his father, and wonder to myself, as I often do, how under different circumstances . . . If his father had not passed away when Jim was only five years old . . . or if we'd had money, or even our own home . . . The view is crisp and clear. Yesterday's rain washed the dust off the city. I am brought out of my inner thoughts as Jim begins to speak again. "You know, Mom," he says, hesitantly, "people think a lot of crazy things about homosexuals . . . it's just not like that."

"I don't know if I want to hear this, but I know I'm going to hear it anyway."

"I'm bisexual," he says. We stop walking. It is my turn to be stunned. I let this sink in. "AIDS," I think. "AIDS." I keep my arm around his waist and we just stand there looking off into the distance.

"Are you ok?" he asks.

"Yes, yes, I'm ok." I reply. But I'm not. I'm terrified that I'll lose him to this awful disease. "Why me?" comes to mind.

"What did I do wrong," creeps into my mind for a moment before I gather the good sense to shove it out. "You

Huizinga in his study of the play element in culture, *Homo Ludens*, points out that the German and Dutch words for duty, "plicht" and "pflicht," are related etymologically to our English word play.

— Joseph Campbell
*Masks of God:
Primitive Mythology*

know better than that, Jeri." I say to myself. "There's nothing you could have done to change this." He pulls me to him and I let my head push into his chest.

"Jim, this is not a good time in history to be bisexual," I say, as I wipe away a tear so he won't see it, thinking how stupid that sounds. I swallow hard and keep myself from crying. "I know, Mom, I know. It's not something I chose. It just is," he says.

That night, back in my hotel room, I am overcome with fear and doubt. I call a friend in Los Angeles for support. It helps. He is my good friend and neighbor, and he is bisexual. I marvel at how, in some mysterious, almost mystical way I always seem to get what I need to carry me through these difficult times, and here I am on the phone with Stephan, whom I've only known a few months, but have grown very close with, pouring my heart out. And at the same time remembering how both Stephan and I had commented that we felt from the very beginning of our friendship that there was some special reason for our meeting. On the plane home to Los Angeles, I am flooded with thoughts and feelings about my son, Jim, and the path our life has taken.

Here we are 21 years after his entrance into this world, and in so many ways, he is the one who is now raising me. How much we've been through. Losing his father when he and his brother were so young, the crazy teenage dramatics. The drugs. How his drug recovery program was the beginning of my real growth, the special people I have met through him. I have learned from being his mother. It has not been easy, but it has created a bond between us that is very special. He has taught me about real love and about personal boundaries and he will not allow me to stay in my self-protective shell. He makes me "come out" too.

Here is Jeri's son's account of the same experience.

My Mom's Visit to San Francisco
by Jim
Age 22

I was hoping for a nice, relaxing weekend with my mom. Maybe impress her with my Victorian flat on Haight and Ashbury, show the architecture of San Francisco, possibly reassure her that things were ok and my life was not a swirling vortex of chaos and emotion. For better or worse, the weekend itself mutated into the swirling vortex.

As I recall, the first night I met her at the hotel to go out to dinner. After the usual mother/son greetings I think the first thing she commented on was my coat. I thought it was simply a nice blue wool trench coat that I looked good in. Nope, turns out to be a lady's coat and I don't look very good in it at all. Minor setback, No problem. Nope, my neck's filthy. We have to wash it before we go out. Minor setback, no problem. Nope, we are now approaching hurdle #2. Tattoos. I made my futile attempt to explain why I got them and I think some of what I did was understood but the shock was too much for her. I was a little hurt at first but soon realized that no mother on god's green earth is going to be thrilled to see her son's tattoos. We have dinner after a while and I think "well tomorrow is a new day."

Mom took the bus to my house and was fortunate enough to get a full dose of the city's homeless problem. She arrived at my house scattered and confused. I wanted to show the flat off to her but she just wanted to get the hell out of there. I even cleaned!!! Oh well, hates the neighborhood. Minor hurdle but at least we're over it.

This is beginning to get long and drawn out. The instructor is probably yawning and mom's grade is slipping with every word. Let's skip the hurdles and get to the high jumps.

We were walking in Fisherman's wharf when the following information was exchanged.

1) My cousin is gay.

Big deal, I already knew that and, hey, mom guess what . . . I'm bisexual and one of my friends that you have the highest regards for was/is my lover. When I told her this, I felt so good and relieved and happy it was incredible. I looked up on the hills and felt a sense of pride and accomplishment in coming out of the closet to my mom. This euphoria was quickly brought down like a ton of bricks.

2) My cousin tested HIV positive.

This shocked and scared me like hell. I love my cousin very much. Without him, I could have never moved to S.F. from L.A. He let me stay at his house for a few days and work for him and I'm so fuckin' angry at that little virus I can't stand it. But not only was I scared for him but for myself as well. Being a former I.V. drug user, bisexual, social deviant was bad enough but this was hitting too close to home. Bullshit, this is my home. It's my family.

The next few hours were spent filling in some details here and there and this is where the good old mother/son bonding and healing process happened. I was in an emotional daze for a little bit after but all in all I'm glad it happened. I got a lot things off my chest and was forced to face some real fears, which I think is good once in a while. But most importantly my mom and I became a lot closer and reached a greater understanding of each other which made the whole weekend worth it.

▲ ▲ ▲

Another effective way of comparing points of view and encouraging children to write is for parents to do the following:

1. Write their earliest experiences.

2. Have the children read their parents' memories back to them.

3. Discuss the stories with their children.

4. Have the children write their earliest memories.

In the following example, Rossana took one of my workshops and became interested in the life writing process. She went home and asked her ten-and-a-half-year-old son to read aloud her earliest memory to see how it sounded. Here is her story.

My Earliest Memory
by Rossana S.
Age 35

I wander in and out of the crowds and feel sick to my stomach. There are people everywhere. Scared, I slowly walk up to my grandmother, who I know I'll probably never see again and I feel very sad.

"I don't feel too good, Abuela, my stomach hurts," I tell her and I clutch my stomach. She takes my hand and leads me upstairs. The marble, spiral staircase seems to be a long way up and my hand tightens around it. Abuela comforts me by holding me, which just makes me feel worse.

People are coming up for a last farewell.

We get in the car that is waiting to take us to the airport and now I start to really cry and I can't stop. I'm not even trying now. I'll never see my friends again, I think, and wish I had at least brought one of my dolls, but it's too late now, and no turning back.

What if I never make friends in America? No one will understand me. I glance over at my younger brothers who are 8 and 3 but they're not crying. They don't understand that we're leaving Cuba, our country, for good. I understand. I look at everyone waving and it makes me feel sadder than I can explain to anyone. I wish we weren't leaving, but my parents say it's for the best.

"Don't worry, Rossana, you'll make new friends and we'll be living in a free country. We'll make sure we write Abuela often." They sound sad too.

The car drives away and I'm crying so hard that I can't even look back to wave one final time. I want to go back, but the car keeps going fast. I feel so helpless.

PS: When I was 9, my parents and brothers and I immigrated to America and left Cuba and its communism behind in order to have a free existence.

Rossana's earliest memory was about leaving Cuba at the time of Castro's accession to power and the pain of leaving her friends behind. Having her son John read this memory aloud to Rossana stimulated a lively discussion about friendship and the difficulty of leaving friends behind. After the discussion, they agreed that it would be interesting to explore his first memory together (and improve his writing as well).

His first draft in Part Three reflects his mother's instruction to write in the present tense. Here is the result of more suggestions from her.

First Memory
(second draft)
by John Lynch

I'm in my Flintstone's pajamas and on my mom's lap hearing but not listening. "John, listen to me do not run in the house," she pointing to the bed end. She goes to the bathroom and guess what I do. I feel that I should not run in the house, but I run like a little Indian dancing around a fire, and boom! Right into the end of the bed. I cry like there's no tomorrow. My mom is still in the bathroom and hears me scream. She comes out with a look of terror and I'm still in pain. She puts a bandaid on hoping it will stop the blood and calls my dad. "Chris, John just got hurt and I'm going to take him to the emergency hospital so meet me there." When I get there I get even more scared. I ask myself: "Will it hurt? Will I go into surgery? Will I die? Oh no," I says to myself when

I go into the doctor's room. He gives me a shot of novacaine and I rest. In the morning I look down at my legs and I say to my mom, "What are those things at the end of my legs?" "Those are stitches. You won't have them for long." she says. A week later, feeling a little better, my mom says we have to go to the emergency hospital. I get worried again thinking we'll go to the hospital every week. I go into the doctor's room and notice that the doctor doesn't give me a shot then I get even more worried. It turns out that he takes my stitches out and I feel very relieved.

This is a nice example of a student's work after several rewrites. Notice that he writes consistently in the present tense and has remembered the story more clearly as a result. Notice the dialogue and dialogue form have improved a great deal. Also he has included his fears in this version.

Writing with Grandparents

Very often the best way for a child to learn the experience of writing his or her life story is through the work of a grandparent. One of the more enjoyable stories I've heard recently came about when one of my students began working with her grandchildren and having them write their stories. Here is her version of that experience.

The Disbudded Authoress
by Mary Hanner

As I walk into my daughter's house on Saturday, I see my grandchildren, Erin and Craig, sitting on opposite sofas, glaring at one another. The atmosphere is tense. I wonder what's up because they get along unusually well. They aren't even relaxing as they greet me with the usual hugs and kisses. "What's going on here?" I ask, directing my question to both. "It's all her fault," Craig answers as he glares at his sixteen-year-old sister. "She has no business putting my belly-button into her stupid old story." "Well, Granny," Erin starts to explain, "you asked if I'd write about my first memory and I did. I can't help it if it included Craig's belly button. I was only 2 years and 9 months old when they brought him home from the hospital. I remember being curious to look him over. He had such neat little hands and feet, but when I saw his crusty brown belly-button I almost barffed out. Absolutely gross."

"It was not!" Craig yells at her, "and anyway you didn't ask me if you could write about it. You don't have my permission and if you do, I'll sue you."

"Oh, yeah, Craig, then the media will broadcast it all over the country. It could make the Persian Gulf and the water shortage look dim."

Craig is looking desperate. His face is flushed. He's trying to think of some way to rescue his belly button. Beside Erin, I see a sheet of paper. It has been neatly done on the computer. "Sorry Granny," Erin says, as she picks up the paper and heads toward the stairway. "I've been doing a term paper on the Holocaust at school and haven't had time to write about my first vivid memory.

"I'll be back down in a little while." She bounds upstairs and Craig glares at her as she goes.

Feeling a little to blame, I try to change the subject, "Grandpa has brought some of his famous chili for you, Craig." I know how much he likes it.

He is able to summon up a little manners as he says, "Oh good, Grandpa should be called the Chili king." He seems distracted now.

That's good. I ask him about school. He replys. Then his face clouds up again. "And to think, Erin has to go and write about my belly button. I'll fix her.

"Erin is coming back down the stairs with a paper in her hand. She hands it to me and I can see that it has been hastily handwritten with many corrections. Now she turns to Craig and says, "Well, Craig, your belly button has fallen into the category of the expletive *&#@*. It has been deleted . . . but at great cost."

Student Assignments

1. Have students get together with a parent or other relative or a close friend and write about a moment they shared in common.

2. Have students get together with a parent and write a parallel experience; i.e., the child's first day in school and mom's first day in school.

10

FINDING THE "HERO WITHIN"

As a perceptive teacher or parent you may sense that children with whom you are working have certain needs that the assignments here do not address. It is important to let students guide themselves by defining their own most vivid memories.

As students write their vivid memories, however, certain themes may begin to emerge that are well worth exploring. Chief among these is the "hero's journey," so well described by Joseph Campbell in his book *The Hero With a Thousand Faces*. In essence, the hero sets off on a life's journey at a given moment in time. She or he comes to a wise person who gives some hints as to how to conduct herself or himself in the months and years to come. The hero is given a magical object to take on the journey. The hero comes to a place of trial where her or his greatest fears must be confronted and descends into the unknown. The hero arises once more from the underworld, reborn and transfigured with new wisdom and new courage. This is the hero's journey.

In ways both large and small all of us follow this path throughout our lives. The question is, do we see ourselves as on this noble path or do we see ourselves as simply buffeted by circumstances?

There are certain assignments students can accomplish that will help them see their hero's journey begin to emerge. These exercises remind students of their personal strengths and individuality. They emphasize the agency students have in their own lives and they build self-esteem.

The assignment that follows should be completed only after students have completed the assignments up to this point and are in full command of the techniques taught so far.

Ask students to:

1. Think of a difficult or challenging situation in your life that you faced well or badly. Describe it in a sentence.

2. Who was around to help you or guide you through that situation?

3. Write a story of a vivid moment in your relationship with this person that is a moment related to Step 1.

4. What were your greatest fears in tackling the problem in Step 1? Describe these fears in a few sentences.

5. What was the character quality that got you through this tough time? (i.e., persistence, tenacity, patience, humor, imagination, etc.)

6. What was your own worst character quality that you had to battle throughout this episode? (i.e., negativity, stubbornness, arrogance, self-deception, short-sightedness, etc.)

7. Write a vivid moment of this tough time in your life. Include in it all of the above—the beginning of the quest, finding a guide, finding a good luck object, withdrawing into a fearful place within yourself, struggling with the problem and rising from despair into activity.

Have students repeat this exercise with other difficult and challenging experiences in their lives.

This exercise can be used as a springboard to explore a number of heroic themes and literary figures. By comparing and contrasting myths, legends, or folktales with the students' writing, you can connect the value of academics and literature with the importance of understanding the hero's journey in the students' own lives.

Another way to strengthen the connection between literature and personal experience is to have students take the message from a fable or folktale and write a contemporary story based on the same message. These fables can be drawn from diverse traditions, for example, The Tortoise and the Hare, Daedelus and Icarus, or the stories of Coyote. Having students draw from the folktales and myths of their cultural heritage encourages them to see how their individual background contributes to the larger whole of society.

More exercises on creating personal myths and developing self-esteem are being developed into workbooks. For a specific discussion about analytical writing, see Chapter 12, A New Path to Teaching Analytical Writing.

PART TWO

How to Use the Process

11

TEACHING THE LIFE STORY
"WRITING FROM WITHIN" PROCESS

*"Grown-ups never understand anything by themselves,
and it is tiresome for children to be always and
forever explaining things to them."*
Antoine de St. Exupéry, The Little Prince

"Writing from within" is an entirely new way of looking at the writing process. It does not invalidate anything you as a teacher or parent may have learned about writing but it will take careful study and an open mind for the techniques outlined here and their effectiveness to be fully understood.

The Process

The basic process is easy to teach and is effective at every level of instruction. In its simplest form the process involves the following steps:

Step 1. Select one's most vivid memory (memories) to write about, then create a picture in one's mind.

Step 2. Tell the story in the past tense, aloud or in writing, then write it in the present tense.

Step 3. Add feelings to the first draft.

Step 4. Get and give some nonjudgmental, corrective feedback.

Step 5. Eliminate any adult-sounding words.

Step 6. Add dialogue during the first revision.

Step 7. Find the beginning of the story.

Step 8. Find the climax of the story and expand it.

Step 9. Add a postscript

The first six simple steps can be accomplished by almost anyone.
What follows is an outline of what you will be doing for the
first few days in the classroom, followed by a suggested format for
the first few days that has proven to be effective.

101

Teaching
the Life
Story
"Writing
from
Within"
Process

An Outline of the Practice of Life Story Writing

1. First assignment—finding one's earliest memory
   A. Prewriting instructions
      1. Discuss storytelling: its importance.
         a. Ask: "What is your favorite story?"
            Response: Note common threads among all students'
            stories.
      2. Discuss the fear of writing (second grade and older).
         a. Ask: "Do you have a fear of writing?"
            Answers: Most people do.
            Response: Encourage students to be honest.
         b. Ask: "What are the fears?"
            Answers:
            1. I try to start; I never finish.
            2. My life is boring.
            3. I've forgotten so much.
            4. People might not like what I write.
            Response:
            1. Explain the critic/creator conflict.
            2. Assure them you will take them through the
               process of identifying and overcoming their fears.
            3. Insist that *once they begin their first draft they need
               to continue on until they finish,* and not worry
               about grammar or spelling.
      3. Have students go back as far as possible in search of
         their earliest memory.
      4. Emphasize it does not have to be a coherent story.
   B. Writing instructions
      1. Have writers tell the story aloud, first in the past tense
         and then again in the present tense.
      2. Have writers notice how much more is recollected in
         the present.
      3. Have writers write their earliest experience in the
         present tense.
      4. Have them write without stopping.
      5. Have them notice how much more is recollected when
         writing in the present tense rather than simply telling
         the story in the present tense.

    C. Postwriting instructions

       1. Provide feedback parameters: "Can you see the picture?" "Can you feel the feelings?"

       2. Show writers how to give nonjudgmental feedback, such as, "I need more details" not "You should have . . ." (for eighth grade and up).

       3. Begin by asking, "Okay, comments?"

    D. Objectives for first assignment

       1. Have writers see how effective present-tense writing is.

       2. Show them that writing in the present tense can be accomplished in the first draft or done in the rewriting.

2. Second assignment—your most vivid memory up to age 12

    A. Prewriting instructions

       1. Have writers write their earliest *vivid* memory. What is it?

          a. It is anything that really did happen to the student.

          b. It may be anything, happy or sad, that the writer can see vividly in his or her mind.

          c. The student should be advised *not to tell something painful* if it is uncomfortable.

       2. Have them write in the present tense.

       3. Have them write without stopping.

    B. Writing instructions

       1. Have writers add dialogue.

       2. Have them add inner thoughts and feelings where possible.

    C. Postwriting instructions (for tenth grade and up)

       1. Ask them to find the first line of dialogue or action: is this the beginning of the story?

       2. Ask them to find the climax of the story: can it be expanded?

       3. Encourage them to add a postscript at the end if it is relevant.

Teaching Life Story Writing in the Classroom

Teachers wanting to use some of what we have discussed in this chapter can try the following in the classroom:

1. Arrange the desks in a semicircle (or two if necessary).

2. Begin with a discussion of storytelling. Is a story fiction? Can a story be nonfiction? What are the characteristics of a story? What are some of their favorite stories? What do

those stories have in common? Ask students if they ever hear stories about their parents' and grandparents' lives.

103

Teaching
the Life
Story
"Writing
from
Within"
Process

3. Ask students how far back they can recall something in their own lives.

    NOTE: at this point it is appropriate to discuss "fear" as described in Chapter 3 in any class where you feel children can grasp the ideas.

4. Have them tell their earliest recollections aloud. (Remember this is not their earliest vivid memory, but the earliest event, fragment, or moment they can remember.)

5. Have them write down the memory in the present tense (very important!). Have them begin with "I am . . ." and give their age.

6. Encourage other class members to describe the difference between the oral and written versions. (Usually the second will yield much more detail.)

7. Have students write the memory down on paper. Urge them not to stop until they have finished the draft.

8. Have students read the written memory aloud to the class.

9. Prompt listeners to describe the differences (only the positive ones) between the oral version and the written version. (Usually the latter has more detail.)

10. Conclude the exercise with positive comments about how interesting even a small memory is.

11. Begin the next exercise on another day, repeating steps 1–10 and asking students to recall their most vivid early memory from age 1–12. Again, they should not tell anything they do not wish to share.

12. Have students rewrite the memory adding dialogue and feelings, as discussed in Chapters 1, 2, and 3.

13. Distinguish between rewriting and editing, and have students edit final drafts of their stories, paying attention to grammar, spelling, etc.

14. Repeat the process until, after two or three memories, students are comfortable writing in the present tense without telling the story aloud.

15. Repeat the process. With each new vivid memory, work on a new element of form—focus, the spine, finding the begin-

ning, developing the climax—if students demonstrate sufficient skills in handling previous steps.

The steps outlined above can be applied to every grade and
every level from the fifth grade to the twelfth and on into college as
well as in adult writing classes. Additional assignments may be
found at the end of each of the early chapters of this book. Much
exciting work can be accomplished by simply using these steps.

Applications

In addition to the normal circumstances in which we might expect
to find life stories taught—classrooms and homes—there are a number of other places where such storytelling might be explored.
Summer camps and arts camps are two such possibilities. Sports-
oriented camps where well-known athletes lecture and tell stories are
excellent places to teach storytelling skills to the young.

School counseling programs are another place where "writing
from within" skills can help students feel less isolated and more fully
connected to the world around them.

One other important occasion for this technique is in writing
the college autobiographical essay. Virtually all of the techniques
described here are applicable to the task. For more detail on the
subject, see the excellent book *On Writing the College Application Essay*
by Harry Bauld.

The following is a sequence of assignments that has proven to
be very successful with elementary, junior high, high school, college,
and older students.

1. Your earliest memory (Chapter 3)
2. Your earliest vivid memory from birth to 12 (Chapter 4)
3. One to five more *vivid* memories from birth to age 10 or 12
   ▲ happiest memory
   ▲ saddest memory
   ▲ funniest or most embarrassing moment
   ▲ biggest adventure
   ▲ funny or sad memory with a parent or grandparent
4. A family history memory (Chapter 8)

The following memories have also been successful with students from high school, college and older adult classes.

5. One to four more *vivid* memories from ages 12–20
   ▲ an intense experience with someone the student's age

- ▲ an experience of separation
- ▲ an experience of a family relationship
- ▲ a letter to one of the student's parents

105

Teaching
the Life
Story
"Writing
from
Within"
Process

I have encountered some differences of opinion within certain school districts as to whether children and young adults should be writing about sad, painful, difficult, or abusive moments in their lives. "We are not therapists," goes one argument, "and we should stay away from areas that we can't handle." The strength of this method is that at no time is the teacher asked to be a therapist; i.e., to talk about causes, reasons, and so on regarding the incident written about. The act of writing about events does more than we as teachers can imagine to help students release feelings and memories. The teacher who confines himself or herself to a discussion of "how to make the scene more vivid and accessible" does the students a great service by diminishing the scariness and isolation of the discussion. On the other hand, we as teachers do have a responsibility to see that students in pain are directed toward counseling.

Teaching Mechanics

One of the great benefits of teaching the "writing from within" method of storytelling is that it puts the task of learning mechanics into its proper perspective. Most of us who are teachers know that children learn mechanics easily if they are motivated and if they learn mechanics in context. The more meaningful the context, the more quickly they can learn.

Perhaps the strongest motivation with life story writing is the need to communicate one's ideas. When a child has a vivid memory of an argument to relate, for example, he or she will find that the proper format for conveying the dialogue is essential for the reader to hear the truth of the argument. So the writer learns that the proper use of quotation marks and punctuation aids the reader in understanding the writer's experience. Learning to view his or her work from the perspective of the reader's needs is a far more effective way for writers to learn mechanics than simply dictating rules.

Your students will learn the writing process most effectively if they are not burdened by having to learn mechanics as they go through the rewriting process. Tell them to write their early drafts without worrying about fixing such aspects as spelling and punctuation. Once they have completed their final drafts, they can then turn their attention to mechanics.

By the time they have finished two or more drafts, you as a teacher may have a great many papers to grade. Don't try to do it yourself. Give students specific elements to look for, such as spelling or certain kinds of punctuation, and allow them to make their own corrections or have them work with another student in a peer-editing situation.

Certain mechanics, however, are very important to the sense of a story. In particular, understanding paragraphing and being able to use punctuation and quotation marks properly for dialogue and inner monologue is very important for students to learn. It is well worth your while to demonstrate time and again the proper use of these mechanics.

One helpful convention, which I have used more and more with my students, is to use double quotes (" . . . ") for dialogue and single quotes (' . . . ') for inner monologue. Many English texts may not support this usage, but I think it makes for the clearest possible separation between dialogue, narrative, and inner monologue. It is also possible to use italics to set off inner monologue, but this is clearly much easier for professional writers to accomplish than for students.

Grading

If grades must be assigned, reserve them for the editing portion of the final draft, or average an A for the composing, reviewing, and rewriting phases into a grade for editing. It is very important that the life story itself receive an A. There are usually plenty of other grades (such as for the editing and for literature assignments) to provide balance.

You may wish to grade the mechanics of the final draft, making certain that students understand it is mechanics that are being graded. In this case, I urge you to assign an A for the story itself.

A Word of Caution

Some of the teachers who take my "writing from within" workshop take a supermarket approach to teaching writing: take a little from this shelf, something from that rack, look over the deli section; they take from it those things they like, while leaving aside the rest. "Writing from within," however, is a process. It is important for you to understand the process as a whole.

Many English teachers, for example, love descriptions of places. Some, I have observed, encourage their students to begin their earliest memories with a description of the surroundings in which the vivid memory takes place. This is the very thing we are trying to get away from in "writing from within"—writing that is flowery, nondramatic, adult, and atmospheric. We are trying to help students grasp the drama implicit in their lives and the sense of story, character, conflict, and relationship that flows from this drama.

Likewise, other teachers would love to have their students use "writing from within" techniques as an adjunct to understanding short stories; they have students read the story and rewrite it using other techniques. This may be a fun and even valuable exercise, but it is not "writing from within." Once students have learned to write their life stories "from within," they can then use the techniques creatively.

107

Teaching
the Life
Story
"Writing
from
Within"
Process

12

A New Path to Teaching Analytical Writing

"People don't use their eyes. They never see a bird, they see a sparrow.
They never see a tree, they see a birch. They don't see concepts."
— Joyce Cary

From the chapters you have read up to now, you may get the idea that telling and writing stories, particularly those that revolve around ourselves, are among the most natural modes of human communication and are probably among the very earliest forms of writing. If this is true, why do we make such a fuss over the teaching of analytical writing in school?

In a very distinct way, analytical thinking and writing assist a person in discriminating the true from the false, the important from the unimportant, fact from fiction, the verifiable from the imagined. Without these abilities, life becomes infinitely more difficult to manage. For example, the ability to produce effective analytical writing is one of the marks of a truly educated person and is one of the most highly prized skills in the business world.

What is good analytical writing and why is it so difficult to get students to accomplish this kind of writing?

My years as a college writing teacher tell me that the difficulty for most students is that good analytical writing takes two quite different sets of skills: narrative skills to make the work human and accessible to a reader and analytical skills to break up the problem into manageable pieces. To learn both sets of skills at one time is, for most students, simply more than they can handle.

In this chapter we will discuss the ways in which those students who have developed life writing skills have a real head start in the process of communicating analytical understanding of events. Then we will suggest an approach to analytical writing that makes the best possible use of these life writing skills.

My proposal—and the work I have been doing for some time— is that we teachers break up the process into two parts: first, learning something of the narrative process through life story writing in the lower grades and then learning the analytical process after the narrative skills.

The students who have done life writing in the manner suggested in the previous chapters will have a good command of narrative writing and can go on to analytical writing and research more fully equipped to handle the tasks. Let's look more closely at how this happens.

The first area in which life story writing skill-building will help is the awareness of the writing process. For most students, analytical writing is a mechanical process: seldom do they confront their fears and find ways around those fears. Even less often do they develop a process for getting into the writer's part of the brain (the right brain), from which come wonderful examples, figures of speech, well-turned phrases, and the like. They also often misunderstand the purpose of rewriting, viewing it as merely a time to correct grammar and punctuation.

Students experienced in life writing, however, know the value of confronting their fears and committing to writing without stopping during the first draft as a way of getting into that childhood as a state of mind, which is beyond self-criticism, and of rewriting as a mode of rethinking and reviewing the work with a sense of what the audience needs to know.

The next area of significance is perhaps the most agonizing task for the student doing analytical writing. This challenge is the task of brainstorming and narrowing the topic. Most students have difficulty choosing a topic with which they can find some personal connection, without simply playing the single note of personal opinion throughout the paper. Objectivity balanced with connectedness is the desired outcome. Students with a "writing from within" background have valuable experience in picking vivid moments about which to write that helps when confronting the brainstorming process for analytical writing.

The third area in which life writing will help is in creating a form that holds the reader's interest. Knowing how to (1) construct a strong, vivid opening to a story with a question that the audience wants solved; (2) create a point of view by using the present tense; (3) develop character by using dialogue and inner monologue; and (4) develop and expand the climax of the story are all experiences with form that enable the writer to keep the audience interested. Each life writing sketch, using the above, is an experience in creating vivid examples of the kind that can be used in a research paper.

On another level, the experience of writing one's life stories is a record of what one has seen and felt and is therefore concerned with in the larger world. To write a postscript at the end of a life

109

A New
Path to
Teaching
Analytical
Writing

A vase of unbaked clay, when broken, may be remoulded, but not a baked one.

— Leonardo da Vinci
Notebooks

story tells the writer that events have consequences, that an early childhood experience will live on in his or her memory and will influence his or her way of seeing the world from that moment on.

With these skills already in hand, the writing student can then concentrate on the more sophisticated, analytical tasks to be learned: comparing and contrasting, classifying, processing, arguing by cause and effect, defining, and persuading. She or he will be able to devote the energy necessary to learning these vitally important writing and life skills.

As a way of better understanding how life writing skills assist the writer of analytical work, let's look at some of the skills developed in the course of writing life stories and see how they compare with typical skills needed in analytical writing.

Comparing Processes: Analytical Writing and "Writing from Within"

Let us now ask ourselves in what ways the process of "writing from within" is similar to, or different from, that of the analytical writing we have explored in this chapter?

Life Story Writing

1. Survey our life's experience; select a vivid moment about which to write; focus on that one moment; narrow the subject so it can be handled.

2. Find the beginning of the story: the first line of action or dialogue (the materials of the story) that causes us to ask a question.

3. Allow the story to unfold through narrative.

4. Use dialogue to help characters come alive.

5. Find the climax and expand on it by introducing minor characters through whose eyes and emotions we see

Analytical Writing

1. Brainstorm to find a subject; find our emotional or intellectual connection to the subject; select materials on the subject.

2. Begin with a tentative thesis, gather materials, reformulate thesis, and supply a teaser that asks a question that points to this thesis.

3. Summarize the problem by allowing its history to unfold.

4. Use quotes to add authority and a sense of actuality.

5. Use a section of analysis to focus on faulty arguments and questionable research methods of the opposition,

and feel the actions of the main characters.

6. Include inner thoughts and feelings to balance narrative and dialogue to give additional insight into different points of view.

7. A postscript at the end allows us to update the narrative, provide information we may have missed, or to explain the impact of the event up to the present time.

8. NJNICA feedback leads to understanding the impact of the writing on another person without fear of criticism.

9. Rewriting is done with a sense of purpose (work on the beginning, expand the climax, etc.), and a clear distinction is made between rewriting and editing.

or to provide new points of view with supporting materials.

6. Develop the analysis to balance the summary (narrative) and expose the reader to several differing points of view.

7. A conclusion pulls the various strands of thinking together and clarifies the impact of the subject on the surrounding community or world.

8. Teacher's supportive feedback leads to understanding one's impact on others.

9. Rewriting should be directed with a sense of purpose, and a clear distinction is made between rewriting and editing.

From this short list of comparisons, we can see that there is a great similarity in the skills developed in life story writing and the skills needed in analytical writing.

Throughout the remainder of this chapter, we will explore some of the ways we can expand the student's capacity to get analytical results down on paper using what we have learned in life story writing. First, however, we must define the form of a research or analytical paper and offer a workable model. We can then look at an approach to finding its content.

Form

The human mind can retain only a small amount of the complexity of the world around it. Like a sieve that allows much of what comes into it to fall through, the mind retains only that which seems to be important to its survival.

Form (or shape) gives a thing certain qualities which allow the mind to grasp it more easily. There is a simplicity and a unity to good form: it is predictable without being repetitious, yet there is also enough variety, tension, and contrast to keep things interesting. Form allows us to know where we are going without being bored as we are getting there.

Basic model for analytical writing

A. Introduction—statement of the problem
B. Body
   1. Summary (definition and/or history) of the problem
   2. Analysis of the problem
      a. Two or more points of view supported by examples and details
      b. Impact of following one or more courses of action
C. Conclusion (including author's recommendations)

This basic model may be expanded by students to include:

A. Introduction
   1. A teaser of some kind (a quote?)
   2. A question of some kind (relating the teaser to the body)
   3. A statement of the problem
   4. A statement of what the paper will undertake, which may be in the first person or third person, depending on the instructor's preference
B. Body
   1. Summary
      a. Definition of problem
      b. History or context of the problem
      c. Return to teaser's subject at the end of the summary
   2. Analysis
      a. Two or more points of view disputing, clarifying, or supporting the definition of the problem
      b. Discussion of the intention, effect, techniques, and impact of the subject under analysis
C. Conclusion
   1. Possibly a return to the teaser's subject at the conclusion of the story
   2. The author's own recommendations, solutions, suggestions

Most research papers also proceed according to one or more rhetorical modes in order to pursue the argument clearly and effectively: definition, comparison/contrast, classification, reasons, narrative, cause and effect, examples, details, process. These modes are helpful to the writer because, by casting the unfolding argument in one or more of these modes, the reader has more of an idea where the text is headed.

113

A New
Path to
Teaching
Analytical
Writing

Content

Most of us find it very difficult to find topics to write about that can be handled in ways that rise above the passions and prejudices of our parents' and peers' religious, political and ethnic affiliations. One of the tasks of the analytical paper is to help pierce through narrow or one-sided viewpoints and carry us toward some clearheaded daylight beyond.

Developing points of view: One way to find the content is to recognize that a great many worthwhile discussions have at their hub the issue of *change* vs. *stasis.* As a consequence, the intention behind most papers of merit is to justify holding to the past by defining it for a new generation or to encourage a departure from a previous mode, approach, or viewpoint.

This tendency to lean in one direction or the other is fundamental to the human condition. The right brain appears to control the functions of the left side of the body (more liberal, change-oriented); the left side of the brain appears to control the functions of the body's right side (conservative).

The following is a list of some opposites that fall under each heading:

The Left Side	*The Right Side*
analytical	synthetical
logical	intuitive
test of truth: verifiable	test of truth: fits into idea
verbal	visual
traditional	unconventional
value-oriented	function-oriented
goal-oriented	process-oriented
detailed	abstract
technical/mathematical	artistic
orderly	spontaneous
extreme—too little movement: *death*	extreme—too much movement: *chaos*

One task of life is to integrate the opposites embodied in these two principles. It is not difficult to see that in every field of human endeavor, we humans learn one way or the other and cannot easily hold both points of view at the same time.

Application of points of view: Content is easily developed if we apply the conflict between right and left, between change and stasis, to any area of knowledge or concern known to man.

Analytical Paper

In Craig B.'s college freshman composition on *terrorism* that follows, the writer is dealing with change, the how's and why's of terrorism, and ways of dealing with terrorism in terms of tradition (how it has been handled in the past) and change (how we may need to deal with it in the future).

Terrorism
by Craig B.
Age 26

The date is September 30, 2000, and the evening news has just begun:

Teaser

Today the President phoned the homes of the survivors of the recent victims of TWA Flight 186. In expressing his condolences, he reassured the families that their relatives "died an honorable death, in the name of democracy, like so many have before." The President then commented to reporters, "It is such a shame to see innocent people die in these terrorist attacks, but it is not too high a price to pay, instead of giving in to these terrorist demands." Is this what the future holds for American citizens abroad? Will they be thought of in the same light as our American servicemen, ready to die for a cause?

Question

Intention

In my paper I will explore the question: "In what way will the lives of hostages be a consideration in future negotiations with terrorists?" I will do this by first defining the terms terrorism, terrorist, and victim. In the process of defining these terms, I will then expand upon their meaning and attempt to give insight into the roles the terrorist, victims, and the public play in the negotiations of hostage situations. Secondly, based upon past terrorist situations, I will show three different options the United States has left in dealing with hostage situations in the future. Finally, I will summarize my findings and draw a conclusion.

summary,
definitions

First, let us define the terms: terrorism, terrorist, and victim. Webster's New College Dictionary defines terrorism as "...the systematic use of terror...as a means of coercion." For our purposes, I have chosen another, more applicable and accurate definition: "Terrorism is the use of murderous violence to achieve political ends that do not obey the rules of war," i.e., the rules laid down by the Geneva Convention. Thus, the type of terrorism we will be dealing with is of a political nature. We now agree, for this paper, that the terrorist's main purpose is to expose and to publicize his cause.

Since we have now defined the term terrorism, we can safely define a terrorist as one who is willing to construct and conduct extremely violent acts as a means to achieve his/her goals of public exposure.

Now let us look at the word *victim*. The Concise Oxford Dictionary of Current English defines the word "victim" as "...a living being sacrificed to a deity or in the performance of a religious rite." "Although the historical development of Judaism, Christianity and Islam has generally moved away from the literally sacrificial practices, this sense of victim is right on target for the systems of explanation and meaning used by most contemporary political terrorists." This is a brief definition, but later I will expand upon the roles the victims play which will provide another dimension to the term.

In order to deal with the hostage situation in the future, we must gain insight into the roles of terrorists and victims, and how the scene of bartering for life is played out for the third, and equally important party, the public. We will first explore the role of the victim.

The role of the victim serves the terrorist in two ways. The first and most obvious is the victim's life, which serves as a symbol of the government that the terrorist defies. Thus the victim's life and the public value of human life are used as the attention-getting bargaining chip that blackmails governments, forcing them to yield, at least partially, to the terrorist demands. Secondly, the victims are used to sway public opinion. If the public can identify with terrorists and their cause, it may undermine the morale and confidence of those in government office, thus severing the trust between the government and the people which is necessary to the operation of a democratic system.

The question now arises, "Why do terrorists choose, and how do they justify such drastic actions?" "What kind of people are these terrorists?" "Don't the terrorists value human life?" In the process of defining the role of the terrorist, I will attempt to answer these questions.

115

A New
Path to
Teaching
Analytical
Writing

analysis

analysis:
intention

analysis:
effect/
techniques

We have previously defined terrorists as individuals who seek to expose their cause to the world. Thus, the bigger the shock, the more widespread the media coverage, and the better the terrorist's cause is served. A Palestine terrorist was discussing the 1970 "Triple Skyjacking". He commented, "It is a severe entry" (a term usually associated with rape) into the public's mind. "For them ... [Americans] ..., it was a particular shock to see the ... [1972] Olympic Games violated so openly and so brazenly. For the terrorists and their supporters, this was precisely the point: They wanted to recontextualize the event and felt morally justified in doing so. Why should anyone be allowed to sit comfortably in his living room while others remained stateless and oppressed?"

So we now understand the methods in which terrorists use the victims, and the media to serve their cause. But what of the terrorists themselves? Who are these people who so willingly risk their own lives and the execution of others, for a cause? Most terrorists are victims themselves. They are usually victims of exploitation, poverty, and constant uprooting. This concept of terrorist as victim is not easily accepted by the public in the midst of a hostage situation. But it should be understood.

Gerard Vaders is a Dutch Newspaperman taken hostage on Dec. 2, 1975 for twelve days by the "Free South Moluccan Youth Movement". He offers this explicit portrayal of the terrorists as victims.

"You had to fight a certain feeling of compassion for the Moluccans. I know this is not natural, but in some ways they came over [as] human. They gave us cigarettes, they gave us blankets. But we also realized that they were killers. You try to suppress that in your consciousness .... I also knew they were victims .... Even more you saw their morale crumbling. You experienced the disintegration of their personalities. The growing despair.... For people at the beginning with egos like gods—impregnable, invincible—they ended up small, desperate, feeling that all was in vain."

The writer explores
the options
available to thwart
terrorists, then
finishes with the
following
conclusion

Conclusion

In conclusion, we have explored and further defined the roles played in the "hostage situation." We learned that terrorists are usually victims themselves, and have been driven to do a deadly act. Secondly, we studied three different ways of dealing with terrorism two of which involved military re-

author's
point of view

sponse, costing innocent lives. And the last choice is negotia-
tion, striving for peace in the Middle East. This writer's view
is that the lives of hostages, and the role they play in future
negotiations, will probably remain unchanged. I believe the
real emphasis must be placed on prevention. For example,
placing tighter controls on the media, thus cutting off the
very exposure on which the terrorists thrive. Secondly, the
highest priority must be placed on intelligence so that possible terrorist attacks may be nipped in the bud. Thirdly, there
must be a drive toward airport security systems for all
airports. This would require the co-operation of foreign nations. Finally, all nations must agree to joint efforts, including, above all, refusing to offer sanctuary to terrorists and
thus indirectly supporting their subversive actions.

117

A New
Path to
Teaching
Analytical
Writing

This short research paper has many of the ingredients which we
teachers like to see. First of all, the subject is narrowed sufficiently
that it can be handled. Secondly, areas of confusion which could lead
to misunderstanding are well-defined. Third, the paper opens in a
way that gets our attention, and the correct question or questions are
asked to get the reader interested and on track: "Is this what the
future holds for Americans abroad?" I might add parenthetically that
the paper was written in 1986 and poses questions which have turned
out to be quite prophetic in light of Saddam Hussein's use of
hostages during the Persian Gulf conflict of 1990.

The author also uses his rhetorical devices to good effect,
defining his terms throughout, classifying the various areas of concern for the reader, supplying numerous examples through quoted
material, and looking at the consequences of terrorism through the
prism of cause and effect.

One can easily argue with the conclusions to which the writer
comes, but of much greater importance is the opportunity he affords
us of viewing the problem of terrorism through new eyes. I found
the definition of "victim" as sacrificial object to be helpful, interesting, and provocative. A research paper may fail in its conclusions to
persuade but may still be of value if the materials from which the
conclusions are taken provide the reader with hitherto unknown
information or perspectives.

Summary

We are now in a better position to assess how the student with life story
writing skills can approach analytical writing with more confidence.

First of all, the student who has written a number of life stories can recognize that good writing results from choosing subjects the author can see clearly and about which he or she feels strongly. The author will have experienced writing a story through to the end *without* criticizing it, evaluating its merits in a review, rewriting it for clarity and impact, and finally editing it for mistakes.

Having placed himself or herself at center stage, the student of life writing will see that every experience told to or written for an audience is going to be seen through someone else's eyes. Life writing experience will help students value the many points of view of life issues and understand that each point of view needs to have its merits and drawbacks evaluated.

The student with life writing experience will have seen ideas that are supported by specific examples of people's actions. Those examples that have an emotional content to them have a particularly great impact on paper. The use of dialogue, like the use of quotations in an analytical paper, adds variety and a human touch to written work while introducing the reader to other points of view.

The student of life writing recognizes the importance of a dynamic opening that is strongly related to the rest of the story. As a result, the student will more easily understand the concept of an introduction that contains a teaser and a statement of purpose.

Perhaps the most difficult part of teaching analytical writing is getting students to explore various points of view thoroughly, to argue coherently, and to support their statements fully. This task is easier when the student has had the experience of expanding the climax of the story by including more action, more dialogue, and more minor characters.

Another difficulty writing teachers face is students' use of sloppy, imprecise, and inflated language. Students with life writing experience have learned how to rid their work of inflated language, paring it of anything that sounds adult, empty, vague, or lacking in color. Students are now aware that adjectives and adverbs are to be used with great care and that active verbs are the high-average hitters of good writing.

Perhaps the most important contribution to students' preparation for writing about the objective world is their awareness of themselves as thinking, feeling, participating beings in life. They have seen how they react in certain situations and how those around them react. They have had a chance to see and feel vivid moments of their lives and have also had the opportunity to step back from those moments and reflect on their impact and meaning. Life story writers realize the importance of their lives and their feelings. In their analytical writing, they will have a chance to look at life more objectively, to nurture their views of the world, and be valued for their thoughts and views about the world in which they live.

Having used the tools of life writing, students are much more fully prepared to handle the writing tasks of research writing and thus more confident as they face the thinking tasks of analytical writing.

119

A New
Path to
Teaching
Analytical
Writing

Student Assignments

1. Compare and contrast two movies or television shows that have some common thread in subject matter, theme, or characterization but differ in other areas such as sense of belief, author's intention, effectiveness, or techniques.

2. Compare and contrast two pieces of music, two musical groups, or musical albums.

3. Compare and contrast two sports teams regarding their playing styles (finesse versus power), attitudes, or coaching approaches.

4. Compare and contrast a human interest piece of journalism with a life story or short story in terms of sense of belief, authors' intentions, techniques, and so on.

5. Compare and contrast yourself, your mother, and your grandmother (or yourself, your father, and your grandfather).

6. Write a cause-and-effect paper about someone who has had a substantial impact on your life.

7. Write a paper about your decision-making process.

13

Teaching "Writing from Within" in Appalachia

Janet Ford wrote me asking about a summer workshop for teachers and I responded by telephone. She told me, in her musical southern drawl, that she and her husband James have been English teachers in a rural Appalachian community for many years. As we talked I could tell she was a highly creative and highly motivated teacher.

"I'm going to be teaching an experimental writing class for kids who have dropped out of day high school and I want to teach them by your method. Do you think I could do that, Bernard?" she asked in her thick and rich-as-honey North Carolina drawl. We decided I could help her best by phoning before each of her sessions to discuss the problems and accomplishment of the previous session.

The following is a blow-by-blow account of these four sessions.

In the year since her class ended, Janet has finished her M.A. thesis in folklore and been hired as an artist-in-residence by a local school system, combining her interest in life story writing, folklore, and dramatics. "I plan to tell the children stories of the folklore of the area which I discovered as I did research for my degree, then we will make the stories into plays. Later, I plan to have them interview their own families and have them write and do murals of the stories that their families tell them about their own pasts."

My Experience Teaching in Rural North Carolina
by Janet Ford

I face the class of high school students. How many times have I been here, I wonder, over my thirteen years teaching high school English. I look out for a face to focus on: bright eyed, alert, a student ready for the teacher to appear. I note the tall, husky youth, directly opposite me. He looks back with the ruffled huff of a professional wrestler, ready for the counter-boast. Two girls straggle in together. They search for their regular teacher, my husband James who is positioning a video camera on the side of the spacious room where I am leading a writing workshop this evening.

Mine is a familiar face in the Extended Day program which provides an alternate evening schedule for about thirty of the students who attend our high school, here in Taylorville, North Carolina. It is located deep within the Appalachian Mountains, a very poor area of the state. They are all "at risk" students, a hair's breadth away from dropping out of school entirely. They are lovely kids . . . but it will be a lot of work getting them to write anything.

The two girls smile and find seats.

I have read *Writing From Within* and the old desire to write, the inspiration of my teaching career, has been rekindled. I have been moved by the quality of the stories that author Bernard Selling has elicited from his students, and this workshop is a testing ground: how will these techniques play among these reluctant young writers? What will we produce?

Bernard Selling is guiding the project from his home in California. I had sent him a note telling him of my interest in his teacher training workshops and he had responded. When he found out I was about to embark on this project, he offered to provide some guidance by telephoning me before each of my four workshops. I feel strong and confident and I proceed according to his instruction.

James lets the camera roll.

"I want to talk to you about stories," I begin. "Have your parents, or your grandparents told you stories?" I ask. A little faltering response. Luke, at the guys' table, feels talkative, willing to participate. My husband is their teacher, and I know that Luke has not attended regularly. I am surprised by the level of participation.

"What about T.V.? What stories do you watch?"

More response now. "Full House," "The Bradys," and "Growing Pains" are mentioned.

"Usually in a story there is someone at the center who is struggling to do good: a hero," I say. We discuss the tenets of heroism. We agree that it has to do with struggling against odds and prevailing, not just for oneself, but for others.

"Have you ever thought of your life as a story with you at the center?" I ask.

Meaningful silence. Aha!

"No one's life is without stories. No one's life lacks opportunities for heroism. You have within you stories that only you can tell, and you are the hero of your life story," I say. This has gone home for everyone of us in the room. If I dismissed the class now I would have achieved something.

"Now try to reach way back for your earliest memory. Take a few minutes to remember, then write your memory down.

This is hard. Several questions arise. I give some examples: an incident involving an old favorite pet or playmate, your grandmother's kitchen...

"Do we have to read these to the class?" asks .... I sense the real difficulty: the fear of writing. We talk about this.

"It's sometimes hard to get started with writing. We are sometimes afraid that we don't have anything interesting to say, or that what we write will be thought dumb." I reassure them.

I talk briefly about the left brain which analyzes and criticizes while the right brain comes up with images. "It's ok to just write. Try to relax. Tell that critic inside that you'll need him later, but for now he can rest."

Silence settles over the room. Pencils begin to move. I am touched by the sincere effort I see. Two minutes later, all but two students have quit writing. Five minutes...the two are still at it. I feel the need to address the majority.

"Now, as some are finishing writing, prepare to tell your memory to someone sitting close to you. You don't have to read what you have written just tell it."

Several choose to read word for word, and stop at that. The professional wrestler is telling his memory without looking at the paper. The two girls laugh loudly and talk back and forth. I go over to them.

"May I see what you have, Nadine?" I ask.

I remember when I was about 5 it was one Christmas and my mom bought me this doll I really wanted. I played with it all day and that night I went to bed and the dog bit the doll's leg off.

I note that both of these girls have used their middle names, rather than the names they usually go by, at the top right of their papers. "Interesting," I say to myself. I look at the other girl's work. Her name is Dawn.

I was about 3 years old and my mom wouldn't let me do something I wanted to and I was sitting on the couch and I yelled out I hate you and ever now and then I still tell her I am sorry for telling her that.

Dawn's mother is suffering the throes of cancer, and Dawn has chosen this memory to recount.

I survey the room. At one table, three listen as one young man reads, then elaborates on his memory. I call them back together.

"Did you remember more as you told the story to each other?" I ask.

They realize that they think and speak more freely than they write. The critic isn't present in their oral telling.

"Now rewrite your memory, this time putting it in the present tense." We talk about the present tense. "Begin with: "I am . . . years old," and include the things you added as you told your memory out loud.

I move around the room helping some get started with the revising process. I pick up a boy named James' pencil and write, "I am six years old . . ." He begins. When the rewrites are complete, I lead the group to contrast their two pieces of writing.

I look at Nadine's story.

It's Christmas morning. I am 4 or 5 years old. I open my present. It is exactly what I want. I play with my doll all day long. I am so happy. I lay my doll on a chair and went to bed. I got back up and looked for my doll. I found it on the floor. The dog chewed its leg off. I am mad.

The second takes are more detailed and more exciting to read, no doubt about it. There is a perceptible little wave of excitement in the air; it's just a little thing, but it seems to augur more to come. In the present tense, these stories are coming to life.

After a stretch break, I talk about including feelings in the stories." How did you feel when you were taken to the principal's office, James?"I ask. He adds a sentence in the double-spaced rewrite.

Dawn rereads her piece silently, then includes a sentence about her feelings: "I am crying now. I feel really bad." She also includes her mother's feelings: "She is crying."

Before dismissing I ask if anyone would like to read his story to the group. With a sense of bravery, Paul volunteers. Paul is a rangy six feet; his dark, liquid eyes make me feel that I am communing with a deer in the woods. He reads his first version to the class.

I remember when I was four and my mom got cut by a piece of metal and I ran to the neighbors to get help.

Then he reads his rewrite.

I am 4 and my mom and I are outside moving tin for dad before he get home from work to surprise him. Then mom turned around and a piece of tin cut her leg open. I took off running through two fields to get help at the neighbors when I got there we drove back to the house and then we took her to the hospital. I was scared.

The heroism of this four-year-old is so obvious it is immediately picked up by the group. It is a perfect ending to this first session.

"Today you recalled your earliest memory. You wrote it, you told it, then you rewrote it in the present tense, including detail and feelings. How do you feel about what you've written today.?" I ask. Several "ok's" follow. This might be a high form of praise from a group of cool, noncommittal high school students.

"For the next class session, be thinking of your most vivid memory," I tell them. "It will be exciting to see how your stories unfold as you continue to write."

Indeed it will.

▲ ▲ ▲

Bernard calls to discuss my first session with the writing group. I find myself starting by reading him Dawn's paragraph and I give him my assessment:

"People tell the truth. You give them a blank sheet of paper, tell them to write their earliest memories, and they'll give you back a succinct sketch of the way they see themselves and the world."

I tell him that the girl whose mother is battling cancer wrote about anger toward her mother, insensitive teachers, and disappointment over a broken doll.

Step-by-step I recount the class session. I read Paul's first writing:

"I noticed that Paul started off in the present tense then quickly slipped back into the past tense," I tell him. "Does this happen a lot?"

"Yes, and it's not a grammatical error but a psychological way of removing himself from a memory," Bernard responds. "Sometimes the writer needs to maintain distance from an event in order to proceed with the memory. You could point this out to him. He'll become aware of what he is doing without your belaboring it."

I read him Rodney's first writing:

When I was about 3 years old I remember going to see our new house that was being built. It looked big, allmost like a manshin. So many poles sticking up out of the ground.

And then the rewrite:

Mom is holding me up to see the skeleton of our house that is being built. I am about three years old. It is very big. It almost looks like a mansion. In a way it looks scary to me. It is so big and so many poles are sticking out of the ground. It is almost dusk and the sun is setting behind it.

"This is typical of the rewrites," I say. "They're more detailed, more vivid."

"Telling the stories orally helps. This is where seeking out helpful feedback comes in. Teaching your students to give and receive helpful feedback is the key to the process," Bernard answers. "Most people think writers work in isolation. Actually, most writers depend heavily on the responses of others."

He elaborates on the teaching of feedback techniques: pictures, feelings, "I" statements, learning to make nonjudgmental supportive statements. "This is where to start with Session 2," he advises. "Feedback is the key."

"After writing their most vivid memories in present tense, including feelings, get them to weed out any adult language that is inappropriate to their age at the time of their memory," Bernard continues. "These items can guide the group in giving and receiving helpful feedback."

"Sounds as though your procedures are right on track," he concludes. It's an English teacher's dream: the supportive scrutiny and encouragement of a mentor.

▲ ▲ ▲

The next day I begin Session 2. I give the students their assignment— to write their most vivid memories. For the most part they have used the present tense. As their classmates read their work, the students listen for vividness of detail and for feelings but, as I move around the room, I am discouraged with what I hear them giving in the guise of feedback—"It was okay," "I liked it." Having given several examples of "I" messages and of nonjudgmental observations, all I hear are bland nonmessages. This will take practice and time. I don't want to hammer away at this concept so I move along.

"Now look at the writing you have done today. You have examined it for vividness of detail and feelings; now I want you to look for any adult language that just doesn't sound right for the age you were when this happened. This is part of putting ourselves in the place and time of which we are writing."

James lets me read his piece.

My most vivid memory is the first time I got snake bit. I was four years old. My mom was working in the flower garden and she dug up a nest of black snakes. I thought they were big worms and I picked one up and it bit me on the heel of my left hand. It hurt a lot but I only got real sick for a couple of hours and then I was just fine.

And his rewrite:

I am four years old. I am playing with some green army men
in the dirt while my mother weeds the flower bed beside our
house. I look up and see a nest of baby black snakes. They
are bigger than worms, gray and wiggling. I pic up one of
the slimy snakes. I yell out and drop the snake. "Ow! That
hurts!" I yell. I feel like a needle has just stuck me in the heel
of my left hand.

My mom turns around; she grabs the snake I was
holding and chops its head off. She takes me into the house,
into the bathroom to the medicine cabinet. My hand hurts;
my mother puts some kind of medicine on it.

I am really sick. For a couple of hours I feel bad all over.
I lie inside the house while my mother tells my dad that I
have been snakebit. He goes out and kills the baby snakes.

Dawn B. writes a most vivid memory of herself at age three or
four years.

I remember riding my tricycle when I was 3 or 4 in the front
yard and my sister and my mom were watching. Then my
sister came running up to me and started slapping my hand
and neither me or my mom knew what was going on, and
when she stopped she told my mom that there was a huge
spider on my hand.

Then she revises it.

I am riding my tricycle in the front yard, and I am enjoying
myself. I can see my mom and my sister sitting on the gras
beside the sidewalk. They are laughing and talking and
taking pictures of me on my new little red tricycle. Then out
of the blue, my sister comes running up to me and starts
slapping my hand. I wonder what it is that I done. Then all
of a sudden . . . .

Her revision includes more detail and feelings, but the concept
of eliminating adult-sounding words has not gotten through. For
some students, this business of eliminating adult language and
finding the child's voice is difficult.

I am touched by the sincerity of their stories. Again, I am
overwhelmed by the way they respond to the assignment with their
innermost concerns.

Angela Dawn presents her most vivid recollection:

I just got home and my brother and sister in law are here they are telling us their baby just died and now everyone is really upset.

Rodney writes;

Me and my sister had a car wreck it flipped 4 times end over end. I wasn't wearing a seat belt. I busted the passenger side window out with my back it cut my back up all over I busted my head. It scared me to death.

Nadine recounts:

One day my aunt and her boyfriend got in a really big fight and he told her he was gong to shoot himself and she cried for a couple of hours then she took an od and we had to take her to the hospital. It scared me so bad. My aunt and I are really close and I felt like I could feel her pain. But she was alright after a couple of days. That's the scaredest I've ever been.

I go to Nadine's table and sit beside her. We go over her story, then I work 20 minutes with her, prodding for detail, defining present tense, and helping her find the right words. Part of the time, I act as her scribe, leaving her free to remember and to think. She works hard at these tasks. Her revision shows a remarkable improvement on the first take.

Nadine's Second Draft

I am at my grandma's house. My aunt lives with my grandma. My aunt's boyfriend is there. They're engaged. They're fighting. He had heard that she had cheated on him. They are all yelling and screaming and hitting each other. It's funny in a way, but it's scary. He pushes her down and she goes off. She is hitting and crying and screaming. I am in between, trying to calm her down.
   "Quit," I tell her. I get them broken up.
   "I'm going to kill myself," he says.
   He spins his tires and leaves.
   More people come over. We notice that my aunt is getting sick.

Time is up and I feel I am in the middle of the session, not the end. I dismiss class without a sense of closure.

Bernard calls. "Hello, Janet. It's me. Your California coach," he laughs. I enjoy talking to him. Working on this process has created a real bond between the two of us. We talk about our lives for a few minutes.

"The process is working," I tell him. "It's working remarkably well. These people are remembering things they had forgotten; all kinds of stuff is coming to the surface, and I feel them struggling for the words to express it. But how do I help a whole class find language. Time doesn't allow me to sit beside each person and pull out detail and vividness. What are the other students going to be doing while I confer one-to-one with each writer."

"Provide a space at the front and center of the room and let students come voluntarily when they are ready for feedback. Then proceed with that one-to-one instruction where others can hear and benefit from what you are saying."

Bernard reminds me that feedback is at the heart of the writing process and that modeling nonjudgmental feedback is the most valuable kind of teaching I can give.

"What about my writing for the kids? I found myself taking the pencils out of their hands and writing the words down. That's wrong isn't it?"

"Sometimes you write for a student in order to break through a block of some kind or other. You don't want to take over his task, but this too is a form of modeling writing. There's nothing wrong with doing some of that."

Bernard's telephone calls tend to buoy me up, to encourage me. He finds the positive in what I am doing and reflects it back to me with the result that I feel freed up, better able to follow instincts with problems that arise.

"Are you writing about your experience with this workshop?"

Bernard asks me. We had talked previously about the value of a journal as I develop the skill of teaching writing. "How's that coming?"

"I'm taking a lot of notes, but I'm having trouble with actually writing about my experience," I tell Bernard.

"English teachers often have a block to get through," he responds." Maybe it comes from years of grading papers, all that red ink," He laughs. "The critic is so active that it can drown out the writer's voice completely."

"Just start writing and send me what you have. It doesn't have to be perfect. It doesn't have to be anything in particular. Try to allow yourself to write, to turn off the critic for awhile."

I realize as I hang up that now I will be involved in the same process I am learning to teach: I will be seeking nonjudgmental feedback, then revising; I realize that this is what I have wanted most in learning to teach writing skills: I will be writing.

▲ ▲ ▲

I open Session 3 with a summary of what has happened in the first two meetings. We have learned to write in the present tense, in language appropriate to the age of the time of the memory; we have begun to include our feelings . . . and to write vividly with detail.

I make the assignment: to continue the process by writing another memory with these points in mind.

The writing is improving. Not every draft bears each of these lessons but the clock now ticks away 10–15 minutes while the class silently writes. Removing the feeling of censure has achieved that much.

Paul's one run-on sentence from the first session typified the student's first draft. Here are Rodney's, Paul's, and James' paragraphs from the third session.

Here is James' story:

I am dove hunting with my step brother. We are loading our guns. My brother is stand off to the side and behind me by about 2 feet. He puts his shells in his shotgun. It goes off right beside my ear when he closes it. I have powder burns all over the right side of my face.

. . . and Paul's story:

It's early. Dad had just wake me up its time to go It's time to go hunting. My birthday was 2 days ago. Meanwhile we dress warmly open the front door and it had snowed. So we started walking it started to get cold it seemed like hours that we had been wealking and once we got home Mom had . . . some hot chocolate.

. . . as well as Rodney's story:

About three years ago I was in an automobile accident. My brother in law and I was going down HWY 16 going to town. We were coming up on an intersection. And a car ran a stop sign and hit us in the front passenger side fender and door, It totaled the car. It hurt my shoulder and head. It hurt his knees and chest. I was lucky I wasn't thrown out because when he hit us my door was knocked open. It was almost Christmas.

The feedback table just naturally evolves during Sessions 3 and 4. It happens that a table of boys close to my podium becomes the gathering place. There are several empty chairs at the table, and after they are filled, the students pull chairs over and sit in a second tier around the table listening as I work with one individual at a time, questioning and answering questions.

I introduce the idea of building dialogue into the stories; it takes with one or two students. All of the students keep writing, keep improving. Bernard encourages me to present each step of the process in sequence, but to accept each students's writing to a great degree.

"You don't want to go at everything all at once, like those papers that look like someone bled all over them," Bernard advises. "Growth is sure to happen if they keep writing."

It is obvious that these young people are more comfortable with writing, more willing to write than they had been. And there is evidence of a growing ability to talk productively about their class-mates' work. I observe a conversation during Session 4 following a writing assignment. Two girls listen to a classmate's work then tell him what they like about it; these are the same two girls who previously had shrugged and said, "It's okay."

I am hearing comments like, "Are we going to write today?" when the students see me, instead of the tense apprehension I had first encountered. We talk about a desk-top publication in the spring. This idea would have been threatening a month ago but now arouses some interest. Gone are the flurry of questions following a writing assignment.

"Do we have to read them out loud?" "How long does it have to be." Everyone knows the process and is growing more comfortable with it.

Paul is now writing in the present tense on his first drafts. This has given his work an exciting immediacy. In Session 4, he produces this vivid memory.

Paul's First Draft—Session Four

Something is outside. I can hear it coming closer to my bed-room and everyone is asleep so I think I'm going to wake up dad. I sneaked and on the way in there is a loud noise outside so I run into my dad's room. When I wake him up, he laughs and explaine what was going on. As he sat and explained what was going on. I found out it was strong winds and snow falling. I went to bed and slept until morning. To have dad take me outside to show me the ice was 4 inches deep and we have no lights. Icycles are falling off powerlines. When they fall they break and that is the only sound I hear through the house.

He becomes the subject of the feedback table's attention as other students write, and another pair of students work together on their revisions. Following a 20-minute session of rewriting, here is what Paul produces:

Paul's Revised Draft—Session 4
Winter's Fear

Something is outside. I can hear it coming closer to my bedroom. Everyone is asleep. I'm going to wake up Dad. I sneak through the house. There is a loud noise outside, like glass breaking.

I run into my dad's room. I have to find him. He is hidden in a bundle of covers. I pull covers off until I see the silouette of him lying curled up on his side in the dark room. I am relieved to find him. He sits up and laughs. Then he tells me what is gong on. Strong winds are blowing and ice is falling.

I go back to bed. I can hear something falling on the roof and windows, but not for long. I sleep until morning, to have Dad take me outside and show me ice four inches deep. We have no lights. Icycles are falling off powerlines. When they fall, they break, and that is the only sound I hear.

The clarity of this piece catches James' (my husband) and my attention. With Paul's consent we enter it in the N.C. International Reading Associations Young Author's project.

Two months later, we receive word that Paul's story is among the winning entries at the state level. By this time, Paul is no longer coming to school. He had married, and is expecting his first child.

"It would be interesting to see what would happen if Paul could keep writing about his experiences," Bernard responded to this news.

It's hard to say what Paul will do with the gains he has made during the four sessions of our writing workshop, but these gains are undeniable. They are gains in insight and self-understanding, as well as in the ability to use paper and ink as a means of expression.

By the time my students and I had met for the four sessions of the writing workshop, we had gotten to know one another through personal glimpses into one another's lives. I felt a growing tolerance in the class: young men had learned of the experiences and struggles of young women; young women had listened to the guys, their concerns, their fears.

This class had not been busy with grammar drills and work-sheets on rules of syntax; they had been engaged in the soul of communication.

I was not separate from all of this growth. I, too, was learning to risk enough to write something down, share it, and listen to another human being's responses.

▲ ▲ ▲

"I got the first installment of your journal," Bernard says. I am both eager and afraid to hear from him. "It's just what I had thought you might be sending," he said. "It's going to be very good."

He then went on to give me some suggestions, as well as to tell me what he had liked in my account of the writing workshop. He indicated some points that needed more thought, some places where I could elaborate.

As I work on a Master of Arts's thesis, which I am now completing at Appalachian State University, I find myself using the concepts from the writing workshop continuously, as well as asking myself, "Is it vivid? Have I sufficiently simplified the language?" I find myself seeking feedback from others. I feel that a career-long habit of self-censorship is breaking up and a new flow of expression is coming forth in its place.

14

A RETURN TO STORYTELLING

Using a few simple techniques, we have enabled students to search out parts of themselves that can provide sources of richness, creativity, newness, and renewal both in and out of school circumstances. These places are the source from which virtually all creative energy springs—the wonder and respect for the child-self that can play endlessly.

We have explored with students ways of harnessing this play-filled energy to express through stories that sense of life as it is experienced by the child. We have also explored ways of expressing that rich inner life of thought and feeling that all of us have within ourselves but often protect from the view of others as our most precious secret.

It is from this inner life that students' happiness in relationships will eventually come. The ability to express one's own feelings and to seek out and appreciate another's is what we mean by "communication." The child who learns to see and write "from within" is far ahead of others in understanding and communicating what is inside himself or herself.

We have also explored with students ways of protecting themselves from the injury of an overly harsh and strident critic while enabling them to hear the tone in the voice of the critic that is helpful to growth. Students have been introduced to the idea that in writing about life experiences and sharing their writing with others, they can expect to gain some insight into their lives.

Where do students go from here? How does life story writing fit into the culture we live in? Virtually everyone who has accomplished anything meaningful in life has a sense of purpose to his or her life. Whether it is from an inherent interest in philosophy, from reading great literature, or from admiring the heroes of one's religious beliefs, we are guided by the quests of those who have come before us.

It is for this reason that storytelling of the highest order—the kind of which myths are made—becomes important. If students write enough stories, choose those that are truly vivid, and include successes and failures that reflect deep feelings, then they are on the path to searching out their own "hero's journeys." This path will emerge from students' writing at a certain point.

What separates our lives from those of mythic heroes such as Percival, Christ, Mohammed, and Buddha, is not so much the nature of the quest, nor the temptations and the journey they follow; the difference is in the challenge that is laid out to them (and to the reader) in the beginning of the tale.

In Percival's quest, for example, the young knight is counseled by his mother not to ask questions of too personal a nature in his travels, as it is uncivilized and intrusive. People will take offense. So when he encounters the Fisher King, who is mortally wounded and suffering, he is careful not to ask what is wrong, and thus wanders for twenty years. Finally, he returns older and wiser to the castle of the Fisher King. He sees the Fisher King still mortally wounded and suffering deeply. This time he asks what ails him. The Fisher King shares with the young knight his deep spiritual pain and, in this act of compassion, Percival finds out that the sufferer is, in fact, his own father.

As students write their own stories and come to see that they too have pleasures and pains, fears and fantasies like the most noble heroes, students will be prepared to see the challenges taking shape ahead of them. They will be able to weigh and assess their challenges as must every hero throughout history.

PART THREE

Life Story Selections

In the following selections the reader will see how the "writing from within" process has brought alive the work of writers of all ages. Whenever possible, I have included first drafts and rewrites so you can see the process of the work.

Selections are arranged in sections, according to the writer's style of development: *younger childhood* writers, *middle childhood* writers, *older childhood* writers, and finally *adulthood* writers, those from ages 20 to 90. Although these last writers are adults, they write of childhood experiences from the point of view of the innocent children they were. They have managed to recover and maintain the child's voice in their work.

You may wish to share these stories with your students.

15

SELECTIONS FROM YOUNGER CHILDHOOD

Selection 1
Boat Trip
by Natalie Chicha
Age 7 1/2

Ecaple days ago we went on a boat to Cataline. First it was smooth and soft. Then when the moder turned on, the water was suft and wavie. I tried to get my ballance but I fell flat on the floor. I went to the caben to put on a life jacket. The life jacket didn't fit I took it off. When we got to Catalina every body got a present I got captin hat. My brother got beach toys. My friend got a doll. My grandmother boughte some taffie for the boat trip. We got tickets for a glass bottom boat.

Click! Click! Click! went my camera.

The boat left without us. We took a boat to catch up on are way back home I threw up. When I got home I felt much better. The end.

Although this memory is told in the past tense, it has the freshness and spontaneous wonderfulness of the young child at play. This is the quality we hope to retain in our work throughout a lifetime of writing.

Selection 2
My Earliest Memory
by Courtney H.
Age 9

When I was about 4 years old I remember that my family was going over to a friend's house and they had a dog. When I approached the dog, he bit me on my upper lip. My dad had a red and green T shirt on with a white collar. My lip was bleeding so when he put me up against his shoulder it became red from blood. They rushed me to the hospital where I saw a boy with his chin split open. The doctors had to strap his hands down because he wouldn't let them touch him. I could hear my dad fighting arguing with the guards to come to me. He got in and let me squeeze his hand when something hurt. When I got home I slept in my brother's room because my sister was with my grandparents. I couldn't suck my thumb.

Courtney's friend, Roz, a fifty-year-old grandmother and student in one of my writing classes, gave her a few instructions—to write in the present tense and use conversation as well. Courtney looked through the workbook and saw other instructions as well. Here is her second draft.

My Earliest Memory
(second draft)
by Courtney H.
Age 9

I am 4 years old. I am going over to a friend's house. They have a big dog.

"I want to pet the dog," I ask.

"Sure, I'll go with you," says my mom.

"Now be care full," she warns. I pet him a couple of times with mom nearby. She sits down again.

"Can I pet him alone?" I ask.

"Sure," my parent says.

So I go up to the dog. He is much bigger than I am. I reach up and pat him but he lunges forward at me and I squeez my eyes shut. He barks once and at the same time he bites my upper lip. It happens so suddenly that I am very scared.

I scream and cry and run to my daddy. He has a green and red striped T-shirt on with a wite collar. He puts me against his shoulder and soothes me with saying, "you are very brave."

My parents rush me to the hospital where I see a boy with a split chin. It makes me feel good that I'm not in his position. The doctors have to strap his hands down because he doesn't let them touch him. I hear my dad arguing with the guards.

Finally he comes in and soothes me again. They have to put a green-felt piece over my eyes. It smells bad.

Daddy says, "squeeze my hand when something hurts."
I fell better (now) that my daddy's with me.

When we get home I sleep in my brother's room with
him. "I want my nightlight in here, it's too dark," I say.

"Fine," my brother says with a sigh. I complain to my
mom because can't suck my thumb.

Here we see the vitality Courtney has brought to her writing by
changing her verbs to the present tense and adding dialogue as
suggested by her friend Roz. On her own, with the aid of the
workbook, she has rediscovered much more about this event, added
many inner thoughts and feelings, and observed wonderful details
("Fine," my brother says with a sigh.)

Selection 3
My Earliest Memory
by John Lynch
Age 11

My earliest memory happened when I was four yers old, still
a terrible two. I was in my flintstone pajamas and on my
mom's lap hearing but not listening. She says not to run in
the house pointing to the bed end. She goes to the bathroom
and guess what I do, I run around like a little indian dancing
around a fire and, boom! right into the end of the bed, I cry
like there's no tomorrow.

My mom is still in the bathroom and hears me scream.
She comes out with a look of terror—me still in pain, puts a
bandaid and calls my dad. She takes me to the emergency
hospital and gets me into the doctor. The doctor gives me a
shot and I don't know what happened. Next day I look down
at my legs and see stitches. I didn't like the looks of it so I
call my mom. She says, "You've got stitches." Then it's a
week later and back I go to the emergency hospital wondering what's going to happen. I get there and go to the doctor.
I see that the doctor doesn't give me a shot of novicane like
he did last time and get worried. I get my stitches removed
and feel relieved.

This first draft shows his mother's instruction to write in the
present tense. Here is the result of more suggestions from her.

My Earliest Memory
(2nd draft)
by John Lynch
Age 11

I'm in my Flintstone's pajamas and on my mom's lap hearing but not listening. "John, listen to me do not run in the house," she says, pointing to the bed end. She goes to the bathroom and guess what I do. I feel that I should not run in the house, but I run like a little indian dancing aorund a fire, and boom! Right into the end of the bed. I cry like there's no tomorrow. My mom is still in the bathroom and hears me scream. She comes out with a look of terror and I'm still in pain. She puts a bandaid on hoping it will stop the blood and calls my dad.

"Chris, John just got hurt and I'm going to take him to the emergency hospital so meet me there." When I get there I get even more scared. I ask myself: "Will it hurt? Will I go into surgery? Will I die?" Oh no, I says to myself when I go into the doctor's room. He gives me a shot of novicane and I rest.

In the morning I look down at my legs and I say to my mom, "What are those things at the end of my legs?"

"Those are stitches. You won't have them for long." she says.

A week later, feeling a little better, my mom says we have to go to the emergency hospital. I get worried again thinking we'll go to the hospital every week. I go into the doctor's room and notice that the doctor doesn't give me a shot then I get even more worried. It turns out that he takes my stitches out and I feel very relieved.

This is a nice example of a student's work after several rewrites. Notice that he writes consistently in the present tense and has remembered the story more clearly as a result. Notice how much the dialogue and the dialogue form have improved. Also he has included his fears this time through.

When your students are feeling abused, bossed, ignored, overwhelmed, powerless, misunderstood, neglected, abandoned, and all the other things young people feel, encourage them to write about the experience, but then suggest they get their parents to write about the experience as well. A lot of misunderstandings can be cleared up in this way.

16

SELECTIONS FROM MIDDLE CHILDHOOD

The following is an example of a story written by a seventh grade "remedial" student as he first wrote it, then as it appeared after he had been taught "writing from within" techniques.

Selection 4
My First Bike Ride
(First Draft)
by Damien S.
7th Grade

The first time I rode a bike was when I was 6 years old on a Saturday afternoon in the summer of Sacramento. When I never ever wanted to use training wheels on my bike but my brother did he used them and used them and that day he finally got on my nerves so bad. Shut up Jason! I bet I could ride that bike better than you can," I said, "No, you can't Jason said, "Yes I can," I said. "I bet you a dollar," "Ok, go for it," I said. Tony, a friend of mine, thought of an idea that might help me. If he would push me maybe I could maintain a balance. So Tony pushed me "Go Damie Go" he said. I was keeping my balance I couldn't believe it I was actually riding without having to use training wheels. Until I turned my head around to laugh at my brother I crashed into my next door neighbors car. My friend Tony helped me off of the front of the car. I kept at it all day until 6:00 pm when we finally had a competition.

After the teacher has instructed students in "writing from within techniques," Damien writes his second draft.

My First Bike Ride
(2nd Draft)

"Dad I don't want to ride with stupid training wheels like Jason," I say. I am 6 years old; its a hot Saturday morning in Sacramento. "Jason looks like a goon riding with training wheels."

Today Jason rode his bike without training wheels. I'm so jealous.

"Damien, maybe if I push you, you'll be able to keep your balance," Tony, a friend of mine, says.

"Go for it," I say. Tony pushes me. I hold my balance and can't believe it. I'm riding without training wheels. I turn around to laugh at Jason and hit a car bumper. I fly in the air and land on the hood of the car.

"Damien, are you alright?" Tony says.

"Yeah, of course," I say.

In one brief lesson lasting less than forty-five minutes, Damien, along with thirty other students in his public school class, has mastered dialogue writing and the form of dialogue writing, and has also simplified and focused the story.

▲ ▲ ▲

Here is a story by another remedial student in the same seventh grade class.

Selection 5
My Earliest Vivid Memory
By Maria Sanchez
7th Grade

When I was two years old my mom was teching me how to use the restroom. Sometimes when she teached me I would be scared because I thought I would fall in. When my mom was areing me up so I could sit on the toilet I would start to cry and I would say, "No!" I don't want to sit down, I don't want to fall in. Then my mom would start telling me that nothing would happen. But, I refused to sit on the toilet.

Then on Tuesday my mom told me that I was going to do it again. But, I refused to. My mom carried me up and took me straight into the rest room then my mom sat me down on the toilet. But I said, No! I don't want to. I don't. I'll fall in. So then my mom made me sit down and then I wasn't scared any more. So then every 4 minutes I would tell my mom that I wanted to use the restroom because I wanted to sit on the toilet because I wasn't scared anymore.

At this point the teacher introduces "writing from within" techniques—writing in the present tense, writing from the child's point of view, bringing in feelings, incorporating dialogue, and learning to rewrite in order to capture more of the experience. Here is the second draft.

My Earliest Vivid Memory
(2nd draft)
by Maria Sanchez

I'm two years old and here I am in the restroom with my mom learning how to use the toilet. My mom is picking me up and sitting me down on the toilet. I'm really scared because I think I'm going to fall in.

"No! I don't want to sit down, I don't want to fall in!" I scream.

My mom starts telling me nothing will happen. But I refuse to sit on the toilet.

Now, it is Tuesday. My mom is telling me I going to do it again. But I refuse. My Mom is carrying me up and taking me to the restroom again. My mom is sitting me down on the toilet.

"No! No! No!" I keep saying. "I'll fall in.

My mom sits me down and I'm not scared anymore. So every 4 minutes I tell my mom that I want to use the restroom because I'm not scared anymore.

In this student's work, the differences are subtle yet important. Once she switches to the present tense, she seems to be *in* the experience much more than in her previous version and so are we, her audience. The language changes in small but important ways: "When I was two . . . my mom teched me . . . and I would be scared.. because I thought I would fall in" now becomes "I am two years old and here I am . . . learning how to use the toilet. I am really scared because I think I am going to fall in."

In the first version the writer is looking at the experience from the mother's point of view ("my mom teched me") while in the later version she is experiencing the event from her own point of view. (" . . . here I am learning . . . ").

Likewise the dialogue shifts are subtle and important. "I would say 'No! I don't want to . . . '" becomes "'No! I don't want to. I don't,' I scream."

17

SELECTIONS FROM OLDER CHILDHOOD

Selection 6
My Earliest Vivid Memory
by Sabina Krich
Age 15

I was almost four years old when I first got my ears pierced. I was very excited but I was also very nervous. I heard stories that they write all over you and then they shoot you with a gun. I was afraid to go. I didn't want anybody to shoot me. My friend's mother was going to take me to the place where I'd get them done. We got to the place and it had a huge selection of jewelry. My friend went first and I was scared to look. Then it was my turn. My heart was beating so fast and I was sweating. I didn't really understand what was going on because I was so little but all of a sudden I was put in a chair and someone was marking my ears with a pen. Then I really got scared. I saw a woman with a gadget in her hand. I assumed she was going to shoot me so I shrugged back out of fear. I found myself holding, actually squeezing someone's hand and I felt two pinches. I opened my eyes and I had two gold earrings in my ears. I was so happy and I started to feel like an adult. When I got home my mother told me the holes were not even and "we'd" have to do them again, as if she was going through the same thing! I refused to go and decided to leave it as is instead of going through all that fear.

Sabina's teacher was a neighbor of Roz G., a woman who has been in my life writing classes for several years. Roz simply instructed Sabina to relate her earliest vivid memory but gave her no other instruction in the first draft.

Afterwards, Roz instructed Sabina to tell the story as if she were the three-year-old, using the present tense and adding dialogue and more feelings. Here is the result.

My Earliest Vivid Memory
(second draft)
by Sabina Krich
Age 15

Today I am going to get my ears pierced. I'm so nervous. I'm only three and a half! I'm going right after school with my friend's mother.

"It's time for lunch," says the teacher. It's the perfect time to ask my friends about it.

"It's awful," says Jennifer. "They write all over you with a marker and then they take a gun and shoot you."

"Oh no," I think. Now I'm so nervous my heart starts beating so fast. I see my friend calling me to come to the car after school. "I'm so excited!" I say. Inside me I feel real nervous.

We're finally here now. I go into the store. I tell my friend to go first. I watch her climb into the chair. I decide to turn around. I can't look. Five minutes pass. It feels like an hour. It is my turn. I am beginning to get wet all over my hands and face. I am naseaus now. I quickly close my eyes and someone lifts me up into a chair. I see a pen coming at me and a pictures comes into my mind of the lady drawing all over me. She puts two dots on me, one on each ear. I get really scared.

"Now they're going to shoot me just like Jennifer said," I think to myself.

The woman by the chair says, "Don't worry sweetie, this won't hurt."

I'm feeling a little better but I still don't believe her. I see her coming at me with the gun. I shrug back. I quickly grab my friend's arm and squeeze it tightly. I close my eyes too. I feel two pinches. I scream because it hurts a little.

"Open your eyes, sweetie," the woman says. I open my eyes. "There you go," says the lady. She gives me a mirror. I look at the mirror. I see two gold earrings, one in each ear. I feel like an adult now!

My friend's mother drives me home. I go into the house.

"Let me see how you look," my mother says. "The holes aren't even." she says. I get scared. Now I have to do it again. My stomach is turning. "We'll have to go back."

I think to myself, "what do you mean 'we'. I'm the one who has to go through that pain." "I like it," I say. I don't want to go back.

My mother tells me, "if you're happy, then I am happy." I am.

In this version, we feel as if we are *in* the experience with Sabina. She captures a sense of the assistant's character—("Open your eyes, sweetie,") and gives us a good picture of her inner thoughts and feelings.

The following is the first memory by a sixteen-year-old girl whose grandmother, Mary Hanner, attended one of my writing classes. Here is Erin's first effort.

Selection 7
My Baby Brother: A First Memory
by Erin Amason
Age 16

To my mind, at age two years and nine months, a small new baby in our house seemed rather unimportant. His only talents appear to be eating, sleeping and howling as loudly as he possibly could. Leaning over his crib in the warm, yellow room, I would meditate upon the unbelievably small scowling face.

People tramped in and out of our small house, filling the rooms with ridiculous cooings and other equally stupid sounding baby noises.

A small sliver of jealousy developed in my mind but still, even thought the jealousy was there, I could not help to feel a certain sense of excitement in watching the tiny human lying helplessly in his crib that will grow up to become my friend as well as my brother.

In this story we do not believe we are experiencing what a three-year-old said and felt. We are certainly impressed that this is a sixteen-year-old with a fine command of language, but the experience feels distant from the reader.

After working with her grandmother for a little while, Erin wrote her next draft using some of the techniques of "writing from within."

My Baby Brother
(2nd Draft)
by Erin Amason
Age 16

I don't see what the fuss is about. He's awfully small, all pink and bald. Silly looking little mittens cover his hands. I sure am a lot bigger, and have a bunch more hair. Hair goes down my back.

He howls a lot, real noisy kid. The big mouth of his just pops open and out spews the loudest noise anyone ever did hear. I never cry, not that much. People come flocking to our house and crowd round that crib of his. They talk to him, the tiny little thing. Don't know why. I sure can understand a lot more than him. I even know my whole alphabet. My mommy and daddy say he's gonna grow up real fast. Don't understand how he will, but I'm real glad. Gonna teach him 'bout big wheels and play parks. He's gonna grow up real good, and I'm gonna help him.

In this version, told in the present tense and in a language mostly purged of sixteen-year-old language, (with the exception of *little*, which is not a concept of a two-year-old, and *spews*) the writer takes us into her world. From it comes a subtle envy and jealousy, an innocent, wide-eyed hope for the future and an open, heartfelt feeling we can interpret as friendship. Here is Erin's most vivid memory, written at the same time as her earliest memory.

Selection 8
My Most Vivid Early Memory
by Erin Amason

Throughout my childhood, I can always remember my two older cousins. With thick glasses and wild brown hair, they would entertain me with their amusing games and tricks. They lived next door to my Granny and Granpa in a small one-story house. Probably their most amazing feat was when they called upon the Indian Rain God for water. Their ceremony took place in my grandparents' garden, next to a gray brick wall. The silence before the ceremony lay heavy in the air. The vivid green color of the tenderly curling ferns leaped out and caught my eye. Moisture danced and sparkled gracefully in the atmosphere. Gravely, my cousins began the ritual. Strange, many-syllabled words poured out of their mouths. Slowly, they began to dance ancient tribal dances and water seeped lazily out of the cracks in the old mottled gray brick wall.

Sometime after my cousins wandered back home, I snuck back out to the garden. It was dusk. Buzzing and whirring insects sampled bites of my skin. Solemnly, I began the ritual, mimicking the exact syllables and movements of my cousins but to no avail, the water did not appear. The seemingly magic powers possessed by my cousins were definitely not with me. Crestfallen, I walked back to my grandparents' house.

The absurd things that I truly believed in! Little did I know that the water that ran from between the bricks came from a green hose that my cousins had placed behind the wall.

After Erin had written this, her grandmother Mary Hanner taught her more of the "writing from within" techniques. Here is the result.

My Most Vivid Early Memory
(2nd Draft)
by Erin Amason

I have two cousins. They are both really old, a whole lot older than I am. They live right next door to my Granny so they can visit me when I come to my Granny's house. Both of my cousins are magical. They really are.

One day they take me out to my Granny's garden, next to a humongous grey wall. We do secret Indian rain dances and suddenly water comes gushing out from the cracks in the wall. "It's absolutely amazing," I think it is the Indian Rain-God who has made the water.

After my cousins leave, I sneak out to the green house garden and try that dance, all by myself. I chant and I dance and I chant some more. I sing to the Rain-God till I can sing no more. I don't know why I don't have any magic. Maybe when I grow up, and be as big as my cousins, I'll be magic too. Boy wouldn't that be something.

This story is much more believable as the experience of a young child, although we wonder just how old she is. We are *in* the experience and awed by the power of the cousins. In this version, however, the writer leaves out a number of important things included in the earlier version: the feeling and texture of the garden before the ceremony, the sense of expectancy, the cousins' wonderful invocation of the rain god during the dance, all of which can be accomplished using "writing from within" techniques while simplifying the language.

Most important of all, the information about the hose needs to be included in the story. Perhaps the writer did not know how to include such information. The solution could be to add a postscript at the end of the story through which the experience is presented from the more recent perspective and additional relevant information is added.

Likewise, this version of the incident could be much more interesting with some dialogue among the cousins and even more of the writer's feelings from one moment to the next.

The following is an account of how Erin's grandmother Mary Hanner went about getting Erin to make these changes.

Selection 9
Driving Miss Erin
by Mary Hanner
Age 72

I glance at the clock. This might be a good time to call Erin. Right after dinner before she starts her homework. She goes to Catholic girls' school and has plenty of that. I press the automatic dial and she answers immediately. She was probably waiting for a call but doesn't seem disappointed when she hears my voice.

"Hi, Granny, what's new?"

"Not too much. I went to writing class today and gave Bernard Selling your stories," I tell her.

"Oh?" she hesitates, then asks cautiously, "What did he say?"

"He was pleased to have them and only needs one more thing."

"What do you mean, one more thing?"

"Well," I'm feeling my way, "he liked them and believes they will be even better if you include some dialogue and mention the green hose in some way. You left it out in the rewrite. Maybe by adding a PS at the end."

"Oh, I would never use a PS, and I hate dialogue," she informs me.

Hmm, this might get a bit touchy, especially over the telephone, so watch it, Granny. There's a thin line here. She loves to write and I don't want to turn her off by being pushy. I can remember being sixteen.

"Well, no matter," I say, "I've been your biggest fan since you started writing your little stories. You were pretty young when you wrote about the wise mother fox who equipped her library with so many books. She wanted her babies to learn to read well so they could cope with the dangerous outside world."

"Oh, I remember...that was a long time ago. It was a pretty cool story." She is laughing.

"It was less than a page and of course you weren't

aware of dialogue then. However, your description of the foxes' den and the reasons for her actions were unique."

"Maybe so, I wonder if I still have that story. I think I'll check it out. I save everything." She seems amused.

I go on, "There never was a time when you weren't in love with your two older boy cousins. You followed them around in true admiration."

"Yeah, I know. I thought they were really rad . . . and I was so naive I can't believe it."

I continue reminiscing, "But the three of you have had lots of fun, making paper costumes, preparing for every holiday and enjoying magic tricks."

"Yeah, the dudes had me fooled, and we have snapshots to prove it."

"I know," I say, "but do you remember how the three of you chattered? You were all so full of ideas."

"We really did," she muses, "it was pretty neat."

"So," I keep on, "when you write about those times, do you think it might be more interesting to describe it with narration, or put in some of that lively dialogue."

"But how can I remember exactly what we said? That was a long time ago and I was just a gullible little kid."

Quickly, I say, "Bernard Selling says it is OK to write down what you *think* was said. It triggers your memory and you get pretty close to the actual conversation. That's one of the most important things I've learned in his class. I couldn't handle it before . . . that, and the present tense."

"Does your professor think you write well?" she asks.

"Well, I'd guess maybe somewhere around so-so. I got started late." I answer.

"Well, I think you're my with-it Granny. You know, some of my friends tell me their grandmothers are biddies."

"Thanks," I tell her. Our admiration is mutual.

There is silence. I wait. Now I hear her say, "OK, I think I want to put some dialogue in my story about the Indian Rain-God. I can do that, and I'll mention the green hose somehow, but I'm not ready for any PS's yet.

"Great, I'll call you again tomorrow and we'll talk about it then."

I think, "PS: Rome wasn't built in a day."

My Most Vivid Early Memory
(3rd Draft)
by Erin Amason

I have two cousins. They are both a lot older than I am. I am five already. They live right next to my Granny and Grandpa on the other side of the big gray wall. I get to see them when I visit Granny.

Both of my cousins are magical. Today Doug asks me, "Do you want to come into the garden and watch us do magic?"

"We will do a rain dance. We can show you how to get water from the Indian Rain-God," Brian tells me.

"Yes," I want to see you do it," I say. This will really be fun.

We run into the garden and Doug says, "Stand here, by these tall ferns and don't move. We will do the magic ceremony."

"I will move this green hose out of our way, we need lots of room," Brian says.

I am being very still. I'm almost not breathing. Granny's ferns are curling all around me but I don't move. It is very quiet. I'm waiting for them to begin.

Now they are starting to do the secret Indian Rain dances. They pat their hands on their mouths and make different noises. They sing and dance around and hop up and down.

"Look!" they say. They are pointing to some water that is gushing from a crack in the wall. Yes, my cousins are magical. They really are.

They have gone home now and I have come back to the garden by myself. I will try to do the rain dance. I'm singing and dancing to the Indian Rain-God. I'm doing all of the things they did. I don't know why I don't have any magic. Maybe when I grow up, and be as big as my cousins, I will be magic too. Boy wouldn't that be fun.

Here we have a nice example of a world that is fresh, new and fascinating from the small child's point of view. The language is believable as the voice of a five-year-old. The dialogue brings us into the story. Some of the richness of the first version is still missing, but it could be included if the child is patient with herself. Likewise, we miss the tag at the end of the story in which she tells us about the source of the water.

18

SELECTIONS FROM YOUNG ADULTHOOD

Selection 10
Pea Green Soup
by Liz Kelly
Age 18

I'm the only one sitting at the table. I'm just sitting there. Everyone else has left. Mom is in the kitchen cleaning up. Dad and the rest of the kids are sitting behind me, watching t.v. I turn around to see what they're watching and Dad yells at me.

"Turn around and finish that soup! You're not getting up til it's done."

I turn back around. I'm four years old and I know I don't like pea green soup. I put my chin on the table and look at the bowl . . . I won't eat it. I don't care if I have to sit here all night. I hate pea green soup. I don't know how everyone else ate theirs.

I've been sitting here a long time. Mom's not done with the dishes yet though because the table is still dirty. Here she comes to wipe the table. Now she's done. They're going to watch t.v. then go to bed. and I'm still going to be sitting here with this yucky pea green soup.

"You can go now," mom says.

"What?" I say.

"Put your bowl in the kitchen," she tells me.

I can hardly believe it! I can get up now! I can go watch t.v. or go play. I don't have to eat my pea green soup! I wonder what's for supper tomorrow.

Selection 11
Sprinkles And Tinkles
by Liz Kelly
Age 18

"Come on! Let's go run around the block!" yells my sister. "Yea!" I think. "I can go too and be part of the group." Everyone is going; my sister Kate, my brother Pat, Danny and Linda; they are my grandma's neighbors and I am going too. This is my big chance to hang out with the big kids since I'm only five and they think that that's still a baby.

Kate is the leader and starts skipping down the sidewalk. It's pretty hot out but it's always hot when we come to visit Grandma. Grandma lives here in Nebraska. I hope we come to some sprinklers soon. Almost everyone waters their laws and when the water squirts over the sidewalk we run through it. (I'm the tail of the group and I stay a little ways behind as we come around the block)

"Oh, no. I have to go to the bathroom. We're too far for me to run all the way back to Grandma's and I know that the rest of the guys won't wait for me. What am I going to do? I know what I'll do. Easy. When we run through the next sprinkler I'll just go a little and no one will know because everything is all wet anyways."

We come to a sprinkler and as we run through I let a little go. But it doesn't stop and I leave a little puddle on the sidewalk next to the water left by the sprinkler.

"Hey," says Danny. "Look, everything's all wet."

"Liz," Kate says. "What did you do?"

"Nothing," I say. "It was the sprinkler."

"She went pee on the sidewalk," says Pat. He thinks he knows everything just because he's six.

"I'm telling Dad," yells Kate and she starts running for Grandma's.

"Wait!" I yell. No one listens to me. I start running after them. I'm going to be in trouble now.

Everyone is sitting on Grandma's porch when I run up. Kate is standing in front of Dad tattling on me. Aunt Barb and Uncle Emil are giving me funny looks as I walk up. I know I'm in trouble. No one has to tell me that.

"Come here," Dad says.

I walk slowly. Maybe I'll be saved if I stall long enough. Mom has that look in her eyes. She feels sorry for me but I know she won't say anything.

"Cornelius," my Grandma says.

"Come on Grandma, save me." I pray to myself.

"Did you go to the bathroom on the sidewalk?" Dad asks me.

I look down at the porch. "Yes," I whisper.

"Don't you know what a toilet is?" I keep my mouth shut. "Is it so hard to come and go pee in the toilet?"

I sneak a peek at his face. He's really mad. His face is turning red and I can see the angry lines in his forehead.

"When are you going to learn, girl? When you have to go pee you come and go in the bathroom and not on the god-damn sidewalk. Jesus Christ." He pauses for a moment. I think he's catching his breath. "What?" he asks. "Were you too busy to come and go in the bathroom?" I can't talk. I think I'm going to cry. "Answer me, girl!!"

"No," whisper.

"What was the problem then?" he asks.

"I don't know," I say. I know that even if I explain that I couldn't come back to Grandma's house to go to the bathroom, he's not going to believe me.

"Pull down your pants," he says.

Oh, no. I don't say anything but I can't believe I'm going to get a spanking right here in front of everybody. I slowly pull down my shorts and my panties. He grabs me by the arm and puts me over his knee. He whacks my bottom hard. (It hurts but I don't cry). He doesn't stop though. I'm going to get a ten star. That's the worst spanking ever. Ten swats in a row. That means I'm really in trouble.

I count every time his hand hits my butt and when I get to number five I'm crying. After number ten, he stand me up.

"Put your pants on, then go change," he tells me.

I look at him to make sure that's all, then I get going. My bum is stinging. I wipe my eyes and try to catch my breath. I race into the house and down the stairs into the cool basement to change my pants.

"Why doesn't Dad like me?" I wonder. "I'll never go pee in the Sprinkler ever again. Maybe then he'll like me."

Selection 12
Going Home
by Teresa S.

I am sixteen years old and I am on the airplane to Peru, my country. I am very excited to see my father. I haven't seen him in ten years. My sister is sitting right next to me.

"Aren't you excited?" I ask her.

"Yes, I very excited," she says, "but I am also a bit nervous."

"Don't worry. Everything is going to be alright."

We finally arrive but it is too late to go see him today.

"Let's wait until tomorrow," my sister says.

We wake up the next morning and I call his house. The phone rings and they finally pick up the phone. My aunt answers.

"Hello," she says.

"How are you?" I say. "Fine," she replies.

"So where's my dad?" I ask.

"I'm sorry to have to tell you this," she says, "but your dad is in the hospital. He'll be there for quite a while. You see, since your dad has a drinking problem, he was taking some pills so he won't desire liquor. But one day he was very depressed and took the whole bottle. He came very close to dying."

I start crying and my sister is looking straight at me, thinking to herself, "what the hell is going on?" I ask my aunt what hospital he is in and when can we go see him. She says the name of the hospital but we can't go visit him until the doctor lets him have visitors.

"Whenever you can see him, I'll call you guys so I can take you," she says.

I hang up and I explain everything to my sister. She stars crying and hugging me. "Don't worry. Everything is going to be ok," I say. I can tell she feels a little better.

Days go by and my aunt hasn't called. We are both very sad because we have to leave in a week and a half and that's not enough time for us to spend with our dad after not seeing him for ten years.

Finally she calls and tells me that we can go tomorrow. "I'll pick you up at 5:00 PM, she says, "so be ready."

"OK," I say.

She picks us up and we are on our way. We finally arrive. We tell the nurse, "We're here to see our dad."

She asks us his name and we tell her. "Hold on, he'll be right with you," she says.

My sister and I are very nervous. Our hearts are pounding very fast.

He finally walks out through the doors and we both run to him and hug him tight. We all start crying and crying because we are so happy to be in his arms again.

Selection 13
Death In The Afternoon
by Eduardo G.
Age 18

Eduardo has been a member of a Latino gang for many years. He is in an alternative high school run by the Los Angeles Unified School District.

First Draft

I remember when my friend told me that my friend got killed. I was asleep and he came over and asked my sister to call me outside. At first I didn't want to go outside but he said it was urgent so I went outside and he told me what happened I couldn't believe what he was saying, I thought he was playing but he wasn't.

After the first draft, I suggested to Eduardo that he rewrite the story in the present tense and add his feelings.

Second Draft

I am 15 years old. I'm sleeping so I'm going to sleep my sister tells me my friend is calling me. I don't want to go cause I'm tired, but my sister says it's urgent so I go outside and ask him what he wants. He tells me my homie got killed I get mad and tell him not to play like that but he says its true so we go to where my friend is at. I'm very angry cause I don't think he should have got killed.

After the second draft, I suggested to Eduardo that he rewrite and add dialogue where possible. Here is the result. (Even his mechanics got better without my correcting him, though I did show him the proper dialogue form.)

Third Draft

I am fifteen years old. I am tired so I'm going to sleep. "Don't wake me up, if anyone comes to look for me, ok?" I tell my sister. A little while later she wakes me up and says, "Your friend's looking for you." "I thought I told you not to wake me up!" I say to her. "He says it's urgent," she says. So I go outside and I ask him, "What do you want?" "Hay homes woody just got killed down the street," he tells me. I get mad and tell him, "Hey ese don't play like that, it ain't funny." "I ain't lying homes, come check it out ese," he says so I get dressed and we go down the street to where my homie is at. I felt so bad that I just wanted to be at home by myself. The next day I was shocked when his brother told us it was some girls that shot him.

Selection 14
Tank Top
by Liz Kelly
Age 18

With my limited wardrobe I don't know how I am ever going to dress cool. It's hard to get noticed being only a sophomore and I don't want to dress like a geek. I stare into my closet; same old shirts, same old pants, same old skirts. I've worn every combination of clothing possible and this morning I don't know what I'm going to put on.

I glance out the window. It's a dark gray morning blanketed in soft white snow. It looks so quiet and peaceful. I turn back into my room and crossover to my dresser. I open the middle drawer of the old antique and absent-mindedly search through the muss of clothing for a possible outfit. An idea strikes me as my hand passes over a dark gray tank top. I reach back and grab the top from the pile.

"Ok, I'm on a roll now," I think to myself. I slip the top over my head and stride back over to my closet. I take the dark brown cords from their hanger along with the light purple oxford. I'm dressed within seconds and I open my door and step into the hallway. I can smell the coffee and toast coming from the kitchen.

I hear the showers running and I know that everyone is up. I look at myself in the full-length mirror that hangs on the rough wood wall. "Not bad. Definitely different, but not ugly." I think. I tuck in my shirt and unbutton the top buttons so that the gray tank shows. I go back in my room to find my old high tops. I want to look casual. I pull my laces tight and then go in search of breakfast.

In the kitchen I run into my older brother Pat. He's a year older and we don't get along all that great at times. "A bit revealing isn't it?" he comments on my shirt.

"No. I'm not showing anything," I shoot back at him.

"Just a little cleavage," he turns back to pouring his milk on his cold cereal. I stand on the other side of the big counter and concentrate on making myself some toast.

"Good morning," says Dad as he comes in and pours himself a cup of coffee.

"Good morning," we respond simultaneously.

Dad looks at me, "Is that what you're wearing to school?"

"Yes," I say.

"She's setting a fashion statement," Pat chimes in.

"I wear it today, everyone else wears it tomorrow." I laugh.

"Go change," Dad says. Pat and I stop laughing. (Pat looks away. If he needs to stand up for himself he does, but otherwise he tries to steer clear of Dad.) I look at Dad's face, searching for a clue to what's going on. I'm not sure if he's really angry. His face is serious and his brow is furrowed.

I don't wait to hear him yell at me and take off to my bedroom to change. I hear his heavy footsteps in the hallway. I study the closed door of my room, the planks so carefully put together yet not even touching, the smooth black handle and the solid bar that latches the door shut.

The latch raises sharply, metal clanking on metal. The door opens and the ungiving wood creaks at me in warning. "Oh, God," I think. "Why did I have to dress this way? Why didn't I know better?" I watch, unmoving, as my father gives the door one hard push and it sails open, slams into the far wall, and slowly bounces back to it's resting place, quivering violently all the while.

In three long strides my father is across the room and he grabs me by the arms. I'm flung from the window to up against the bunk bed. My head cracks soundly against the old wood frame of the upper bunk but I dare not reach my hand up to try and soothe away the pain.

"You are not wearing that to school," he screams. "Don't you have any god-damn decent clothes?"

"No," I want to scream back. "I'm trying to make do with the little that I have," but I don't scream it. I know I have to take his shit. He points his finger at me. His hand is becoming worn with age but I know how strong that hand still is. He jabs me forcefully in the chest.

"This is my house! I make the rules and if you are going to live here then you better damn well follow them." His finger is the only thing that keeps his fist from hitting me again and again as if trying to stay in beat with my pounding heart.

"I won't cry," I tell myself. I bite my lip and hold back the tears. "I'll change my clothes, and I'll follow his rules, and I'll take his shit, but he is never ever going to see me cry because of him." I look him in the eye and listen to every word he says. I ignore the shaking of my legs and the tears welling up in the back of my eyes. He gives me one hard shove and I sit down hard on the bottom bed.

"No daughter of mine is leaving this house dressed like a whore!!" he says with finality and storms out of the room. I sit on the bed not daring to move yet still shaking like a leaf.

"I am not crying," I say to myself over and over. "It's o.k." I take a deep breath. "I'll leave. I go live with someone else. I'll runaway. I will get out of here somehow, someway." I slowly bring myself to my feet and walk to my closet. "He doesn't care. He never has and never will. Just wait 'til I'm gone."

I grab a different shirt from its hanger and change the shirt I have on. Then I take off my shoes and change my pants for jeans. Off in the distance I hear a door open and then slam shut again. "Good. He's gone to school." I think. I open my door and step into the hallway to check myself in the mirror.

Pat comes from the kitchen and watches for a moment as I straighten myself in the mirror.

"The shirt really was revealing," he says.

"It was not that revealing," I argue.

"Liz, if I was Dad, I wouldn't let you dress like that either. You let your boobs hang out and you'll have every redneck in the school staring at your chest," Pat tells me.

"I am not that big," I say. "You have big boobs," he says and walks past me into the bedroom.

"Some free country we live in. I can't even dress the way I want to. I was hardly dressed like a whore. Dad can say what he wants and do what he likes but as soon as I'm gone I'm never speaking to that bastard again." I talk to myself tough, and I act tough, but my insides feel like spaghetti. I go back to the kitchen acting as normal as I possibly can.

I eat my toast, trying to keep from choking. My younger brother Michael looks at me from across the table with his big brown eyes and just shakes his head. He's three years younger than I am but smart for his age. He believes in keeping his nose clean. He reads his books and does his homework.

I finish getting ready for school and step out the door into the icy cold morning. I slide my feet across the frosty porch and down the slippery wooden steps. Crunch, crunch, crunch. My footsteps are the only sounds in the snow. Thud, thud, thud. In my mind I hear his finger banging into my chest.

"Damn it. I am not going to cry. I have my pride and if I let this little incident get to me then I'm never going to survive the real world." The school isn't too much further. The gray paved road stretches forever though, right up to the gray sky. When I reach the school door, I take a deep breath, trying to calm my shaken nerves.

"I pray to god I don't run into him," I tell myself. It really sucks that my dad teaches at the high school. I don't see him. I dump my stuff in my locker and go to join my friends in the hall hangout. I see my friends, Lori and Joszi.

"Hi, guys," I say.

"Hey Liz, how's it going?" they ask.

"Fine," I reply. Lori gives me a funny look. I'm trying as hard as I possibly can to hold back the tears that seem to be forming in my throat.

"Liz, what's wrong?" Lori asks.

"Nothing," I say as I turn and quickly walk away so they won't see me crying. I only take a few steps then I dry my eyes and turn and walk back.

"Liz, there's something wrong," Lori says. She puts her arm around me and guides me into the counselor's office. Mr. Cothern, the counselor, gives me a knowing look. I've been here before. Lori sits me down in a chair and I put my face in my hands and cry.

Lori leaves to go to class and Cothern and I go into discussion. "I can't live with my father anymore," I tell Cothern. "I can't handle it." Cothern gives me a serious look.

Well, as serious as his looks ever get. Mr. Cothern is a tall man that reminds me of a character out of a cartoon strip. His eyes are always laughing and I don't think he takes me seriously.

"Cothern, I'm serious." I try to convince him.

"Liz, your dad isn't going to move out, and if you stick around things are going to get better. You can work them out."

"Fine," I say. I sit and listen a while longer then I go back to class. I know, only too well, that things are not going to change.

Bernard Selling's PS: Shortly after this incident, which occurred when Liz was sixteen, she dropped out of school, left Wyoming and came to Southern California where she began working as a live-in housekeeper. On her one morning off each week, she came to one of my life story writing classes.

Now twenty and living in Santa Cruz, California, Liz tells me that writing her stories has not only clarified her feelings but has helped other members of the family begin to express their feelings as well. She tells me that at long last the whole family is beginning to deal with her father's rage and with the alcoholism that has often unleashed it.

19

SELECTIONS FROM ADULTHOOD

Selection 15
The Indian Boys
by Bennie Trenkamp
Age 80
(as told to Margaret T.)

I am seven years old in Spearville, Kansas on the farm with
my grandpa. It is 1918. I am helping ride herd on the cows.
One day we are about seven miles from home when here
come five Indian boys about my age riding up. I think, "Oh,
they want to play with me," in the evening before it gets
dark. They say something I cannot understand. "You want to
play?" I ask. They look at each other. They cannot understand me. Then two of them one on each side of my horse
take my reins and lead me away with them. I think we are
going to play a game or something, but instead they lead me
to the Indian camp which is three or four miles away. There's
always a cowhand overseeing me and the cows wherever I
am, so I never feel alone or a afraid while I am doing
something with or for my grandpa . . . up to now. When they
lead me into camp, they have me get off my horse. Then they
lead me over to a shaffel where they hung their clothes and
hides to dry. Then they tied my thumbs with wang leather,
as I am standing up. They tie me to the shaffel with my arms
up. My feet are on the ground. Then they leave me alone. I
don't know how long I am there. It seems like hours and I
cannot get loose. And it is getting dark. I scared. I look up
and there is Grandpa coming after me. He rides right into the
Indian camp and gets the chief out there. Grandpa can speak
their language. He tells them what happened to me while I
was watching cows for him. Grandpa is big and strong, half
a head taller than anyone else. He says something to their
chief in their language. The chief says, "Hu . . hu . ." and has
the boys bring my horse back to me. As we leave, Grandpa

tells me, "They were playing Indian games with you. They're Cherokee Indians. They're the friendliest of any of 'em and won't hurt you." "Grandpa," I say, "I sure was glad you came after me an I'm glad you always got one of the cow hands lookin' after the herd and me wherever I am." PS: Up to this day I still have the scars on my thumbs where they tied the wang leather there when I was a little boy helping Grandpa out with the cows.

Selection 16
First Kiss
by Diane Hanson
Age 45

I just got home from jr. high and am hanging around the kitchen trying to work up the nerve to tell my Mom something. Every once in a while she will look at me, wondering what I am doing. I should have said something sooner because now it is harder to tell her. She knows I have something important to say. The longer I put this off, the worse it is. "Mom," I try to start. She looks at me. "Well, what is it?" "Mom," I start again, " . . . Tommy has asked me to go steady and I have said yes." She looks surprised. "Why on earth would you want to tie yourself down to one boy when you are only 14." "Because none of the other boys are asking me to go anywhere, so I may as well." My answer has stopped her, she has no further argument. "So, Mom, he will be here at 4 PM to give me his ring." She shrugs, says nothing more, so I leave the kitchen feeling relieved. At four Tommy rings the door bell. He is about my height, short brown crew cut, and blue eyes. He is nice and talks to me alot at school. It is summer time so we sit outside on the front porch. He puts his arm around me. It feels heavy and uncomfortable. "So will you be my steady?" he asks. "Sure," I answer. I wonder what the big deal is. After all, this has been decided already and he is here to seal the pact by giving me his ring. "Here," he says putting the ring in my hand. I take the neck scarf off I wore for the occasion and tie a knot through the heavy man's ring. Then Tommy ties it behind my neck as I hold my hair up. He smiles at me and I smile at him. His arm plunks down on my shoulder again. His face gets closer to mine. I can see a zit near his nose! "We should kiss now," he informs me. "Kiss? Kiss?!!" I think. "Somehow I know that his kissing me was part of the deal." His face gets closer to mine.

I wonder if my nose is going to land on that zit? I feel very stiff and uncomfortable. His breathing is very heavy and his breath smells bad. Plunk, his lips land on mine. My eyes are open so I can see that his are shut. "Why are they shut?" I wonder. His lips stay on mine and I wait impatiently until he is done. He pulls back really smiling now. I am glad he is done so I am smiling too. "Well, I will see you at school tomorrow." he says as he gets up to leave. "Sure, I'll see you then." He leaves and I re-enter the house thinking, "I hope he isn't going to kiss me again tomorrow. It was awful wet and messy. The next day he did kiss me, so I gave back the ring so that he wouldn't kiss me anymore.

Selection 17
The Overhead Bridge
by Edward White

I love to walk to the Post Office and pick up our mail. The Post Office is about two miles from Granny's house in downtown Ruston, Louisiana. Our box number is Box 107. I remove the mailbox key from the string around my neck and open our mailbox. "Ahh, Ooooweee!" I yell to myself. I count to myself. "Granny sure has a lot of mail today." Because my mother is a school teacher and helps me with all of my school work along with her two youngest sisters, "Baby Lowell" and Sally Brooks, I learn to read very good and I have a very good knowledge of words and a better than most kids' understanding of the language. With three good teachers any kid can learn fast, at least something. Since I was three years old, I read better than most kids. I am seven now. "Oh! Here is a letter my Mother Dear; wonder if she has any money in it for Granny and me? One is from Aunt "Brookside," another from "Baby Lowell." I bet they want something. They are away at school, college or something!"

"Ooooo, here's one from Aunt Anna. She hasn't written in a long time; this one is from "Aunt Tee." (Lucyellen). I don't know why we call her "Aunt Tee." And here is the last one—a letter from good old Uncle Charlie, Granny's oldest son. This should make my grandmother happy, six letters in all, but I know what she will say when I get home. "Sonny, we didn't get no mail from "little Brother." Everyone calls Uncle John Glover Harvey either "Little Uncle" or "Little Brother" or the "Baby Boy." "Lawd! Lawd! Why don't he ever write just to let me know how he is getting along. I keep so worried all of the time wondering if something has happened to him. My baby got his leg cut off riding them freight trains when he weren't but nine years old, and has been a-hoboin' ever since, just ridin' the rails all over this land. He's been in every state in the country, I 'spect. Lawd! Lawd! Have mercy!"

It seems that Granny would know by now that "Little Uncle" only writes to her or anyone else when they needs some money or something. We see him once in a great while. One day "Little Uncle" will come home for a day or so, then he will leave just like he came, like Santa Claus. Only "Little Uncle" won't bring anything but himself. "I just cain't stand to hear a freight train whistle blow. I just have to put on my travelin' clothes and go." That's what "Little Uncle" tells everyone.

"Hey there boy!" One of the mail clerks hollers at me as I am walking out the door of the Post Office. "Tell your grandma that sure was a good chocolate cake she mailed to her daughter. Be sure to tell her to make a bigger cake next time so everybody in OUR Post Office can get some." He laughs real loud. "HEH! HEH! HEH!" I turn and look back at him. He kind of throws back his head a little. He has a very RED face, a big throat, and he is the one I have seen up close with the wrinkles in his neck like a turkey. I say nothing as I wonder to myself, "Is he one of the kinds of people that the 'rich white' people call "cracker trash?"? I am getting close to the OLD OVERHEAD BRIDGE. It is made and shaped like a BIG RAINBOW. I have to cross the bridge going to and from the Post Office. Trains going out of and coming into town pass under the Overhead Bridge.

Sitting on an old cane-bottom chair at the bottom of the crossing is a very old, gray head white man. He is talking to a very big white boy as he kind of rocks back and forth in his chair. As I get near them I see that the boy is about "Baby Lowell's" age, around seventeen or so, and he is not old and ugly looking like the old man. The boy is bare-headed. His hair is short, light-colored and sandy-looking. The old man has on a dirty pair of raggedy-looking overalls and an old straw hat that has a hole in it. Neither of them have any shoes on, just like me. Because both the old man and the boy are poor-looking, I think that they must be nice and not mean white people, like that old Post Office clerk who ate up "Baby Lowell's" chocolate cake that Granny had baked and mailed to her.

As I walk by the two, the old man and the boy, I kind of smile at them, thinking they are nice people.

"Wait a MINUTE!" shouts the big boy real mean and ugly-like. "WHATCHALL EN YOU HANES?" He drawls out nasty and slow.

"It's mail for my Granny," I whisper, kind of scared but not too much because the ugly old man is nearby. "Gimme dat dare mail," he drawls, snatching the mail from my hand. I look kind of long at the ugly old man and wait for him to make the big boy give me back our mail. Being little and the boy being big, I know that the ugly old man will be on my side and will make the boy give me back my mail. The mean old gray-headed man just GRINS HIS TOOTHLESS GRIN and watches me. Tobacco or snuff spit drools down the corner of his UGLY MOUTH which seems to sit almost in the middle of an ugly, odd shaped face. He has greenish bird-eyes that shift from me to the big boy. He reminds me some of a chicken hawk.

The big boy now begins to open my mail. He takes his time and reads the letters very slow to the old man, and they laugh at anything they think is funny. Because Granny cannot read or write, all the family members know that I read the mail to her. They write large and clear, and are sure to use words that I can understand.

The big boy stumbles across a word that he cannot pronounce. It is an easy word, at least for me. He begins to stumble and spell out the word. "Let me see," he stumbles, "Ppp-rrr-o-gram? Prigrin-UH! Wonder what the hell is that?"

"It's not prigrin. It's PROGRAM. Don't you know what a program is?" I ask him.

"LISTEN HEAH! YOU SHUT UP NIGGER! Don't you even darc to make a fool out of a white man! Do ya heah me, Nigger boy?"

"Yes!" I answer.

"WHATTA you mean YES. Don't you know you be talkin' to a white man? Yo folks better teach you yo manners 'fo you grow up an gits lynched. We love ta have neck tie parties for you smart uppity niggers. They want to teach you to grow up RIGHT and RESPECT WHITE FOLKS! YOU HEAH ME, BOY?" "Yes, sir," I answer. Tears begin to run down my face to the hot ground. It is not the word NIGGER or saying YES SIR that makes me cry—It's reading of our MAIL—OUR MAIL—GRANNY'S MAIL. He puts all of the mail in the right envelopes. I think he is trying to let me know that he can read as well as I can, but I know that he can't. He gives the mail back to me. "NOW YOU GIT!!! I WANTCHA TA GIT!! GIT TA RUNNIN'! DON'T YA DARE

LOOK BACK!" He slaps his hands hard and loud, and kicks at me. I jump back. He misses. I run almost all the way home. I am mad and scared as I run home. Two miles is a long way for a seven-year old, so I run some but trot most of the way. I think of the old man and the big boy. How they stink. I think it is a very hot day and both of them are mean and stinking. But the "UGLY OLD MAN STINKS WORST THAN THE BOY" I say to myself. "Maybe it's because the old man has been meaner and stinking longer than the boy." There is a difference between the postal clerk and the mean two. The postal clerk must be what rich people call "cracker trash", and the mean two must be what rich white people call "POOR WHITE TRASH". Granny works for a real rich white lady sometimes, and Granny tells me that when Mrs. Satterfield leaves her home for any reason, she tells Granny, "Now Lucinda, effen any niggers at all come by heah a-beggin for food while I'm gone, I want you to be sure and feed the niggers but effen any poor white trash come by heah for anything at all, I want you to call Sheriff Thigpen and get them the hell away from my premises. Don't give THE TRASH a damned thing! Let the trash starve to death! That's what they deserve. They been free all their born no account days. Now do you heah me Lucinda?" "Yes'm I heah you, Miss Satterfield." One day I asked Granny, "What do you do when the beggars come by, Granny? Do you do what Mrs. Satterfield tells you to do?" "GOD DON'T LOVE UGLE, CHILE. I just feeds them all who comes by begging for food. I feeds them all, black and white alike."

I am finally home. It seems like I have been gone all day. I hurry into the house. Granny can tell I have been crying, and I am a little out of breath. "Why what's the matter, Chile? What's the matter? Tell your Granny."

I tell Granny all about it. The South bein' what it is, nothing can be done about what happened to me. Granny pulls me to her and whispers, "We will just have to take it to the Good Lord in prayer. He will wipe away all tears and he will wash away all sorrow. Let us try and forget about it. God changes things, Sonny."

I think to myself just before getting ready to go to bed, "Granny is right. Granny is always right. My Granny is always RIGHT? There are no more tears, and no sorrow and no anger.

Now I look back and laugh at it all—But how CAN I FORGET?

Selection 18
Leaving The Plantation
by Florence M.
Age 65

"It's feeding time," I can hear my father yell after he comes home from working the fields. My younger brother and I tag along to help care for the animals. Milking cows, feeding chickens, and slopping hogs is just another job to be done as part of our daily farm life.

We grow ever so tired and weary of working the plantation from sun up to sun down. Oh, how we long for a better life. My father and brothers often complain of getting overheated in the corn crops, or having to plow the fields in the heat of the southern sun. Time and time again things become almost unbearable and my brothers talk of leaving the plantation one by one. We can always make ourselves feel better by vowing to save enough money to buy our very own house.

Poor crops and the low price of cotton make this almost impossible, because all sharecroppers are paid at the end of each year.

For many years my father is given a drink of whiskey and a pat on the back and told, "Sorry Henry but you did not make it out of debt this year."

"Those words would always make my heart ache," my father says.

The land owner attempts to pacify him by saying, "Now, Henry if you and your children work hard, I am sure you will make it out of debt by next year."

My father tries to explain to him the things that we need just to be able to exist.

"Don't worry about a thing." the land owner says to him. "Haven't I always taken care of you and your little colored children? I have made arrangements at the general store and you can get a few things that you need there."

My father says, "yes sir, Mr. Temp."

Mr. Temp places a big cigar in his mouth, unscrews the cap on the whiskey bottle. "Have another drink Henry," he says. "I look forward to drinking with you good colored folks at the end of the year." Sometime during the early forties, just when we think our dreams are never going to become a reality, farmers all over the south have a good year, crops are excellent, the price of cotton goes extremely high. There has been some talk among the sharecroppers that absolutely no one is going to be left in debt this year.

They are right. The land owner comes and pays my father more money than we have ever seen in our lifetime. We have more than enough to buy our own house in the little country town of Keo, Arkansas, located twenty-five miles away from our home, where we are sure to live a more progressive life style.

Now that we have the money I am waiting for my parents to say that we will soon be moving any day. We know that my father is a bit hesitant but we do not know why.

Then one day without warning he comes home with a big car—long, black, shiny, and new.

He has a big smile on his face. When we see that big car we have smiles on our faces too. My mother meets him at the door with no smile on her face.

"Henry, what is this?" my mother asks.

"Well, Florence, as you cans see its a car." my father answers.

"What about our house?" she asks. "We can get our house next year," my father replies.

Somehow my mother is able to contain her tears, but she is not able to maintain her sanity.

"I can't wait another year!" she shouts and glares at my father.

"If it's left up to you we will never get off this plantation."

My mother starts running around kicking chairs and pounding on tables. Many angry words are flowing from her lips. By now any smiles that we have had on our faces about that car have already faded. Spellbound, we sit, watch and listen, as our mother verbally fights with our father over spending the money on a car that we were going to use for our house. She actually accuses him of being afraid to leave the plantation. She tells him that he had to have received encouragement from the overseer to do such a thing. My father has little to say in defense of himself. I don't think there's anything he can say.

When it is all over, my mother has succeeded in painting such a clear negative picture of my father even we can see it. She has made him look as if he has less than a bird's brain. We sit without movement, looking at him with big sad, glassy eyes, feeling little or no sympathy for him. It is obvious whose side we are on.

The next few days at our house are sheer gloom. The gloom is lifted when my mother takes matters into her own hands and announces that along with the left over money we are going to sell the animals to help make payment on our new house. My older sister and brothers are happy. My younger brother and I are oh, so sad, because we grew up with most of those animals that she is talking about selling and to release them isn't going to be easy.

These animals that are being sold are like members of our family. For example old Rose, our brown and white cow. She is gentle as a lamb. She had never kicked over a bucket of her milk in her life. Old Rose is first to go. Then there is Fat Sam, the hog. We had raised Fat Sam from a little pig. Sam is so greedy he used to slurp all the slop from the other hogs and squeel long and hard if we did not give him more. As much as we complain about him we can not hide the pain when it is fat Sam's turn to leave. Tears roll from my face as I say goodby to most of the animals I have known as a child. I have these same uncontrollable tears when it is time to close the front door on the old plantation farm house that had been my birth place and the only home I have ever known.

Selections from Adulthood

GLOSSARY

ADJECTIVES — are words that fill in the picture of characters, actions, and objects. "He was a tall, fat man with droopy eyelids and dirty overalls." In life writing, we try to reduce the number of adjectives that cluster around an object. Instead we create separate sentences that give another view of the object or character. "He stands half a head above everyone else. His stomach hangs over his belt like he has a bowling ball tucked inside his shirt. His eyelids droop like he's half asleep but I feel them following me everywhere I go."

ADVERBS — are words (usually words ending in "-ly") that fill out the actions. "He walked slowly down the street, careful to make no noise." In life writing, we try to get rid of adverbs because they often shade actions that do not need shading. "I cried loudly," or "He ran swiftly," or "She crept stealthily through the brush." In each case, we did not need the adverb. "I cried," "He ran," and "He crept through the brush," all do just fine.

BALANCE — In good writing, we seek a balance of narrative, dialogue, and inner monologue. In this way, the writer can convey to the reader what is going on in the outer world of action, events, and emotions and in the inner world of the central character's thoughts and feelings.

BELIEF — is the way most of us judge the truth of a story. If it sounds believable, we tend to accept it as true. One of the goals of almost any writer is to get the reader to accept the characters and events in a story as believable. Almost every reader comes to reading stories or watching stories on television with a certain disbelief. This is healthy. The job of the writer is to get the readers to suspend this natural disbelief, to help the reader enter the world the writer is creating and to keep the reader there for the duration of the story.

CENTRAL CHARACTER — is the person around whom the events in the story are woven. In life story writing, the central character is often the narrator of the story. One of the tasks of the effective writer of life stories is to create an interesting character through whose eyes we see the actions, yet who may not know everything that is happening in the story. For example, minor characters may say interesting things that the central character hears but does not understand. In this way the narrative moves forward without the central character knowing everything. For example:

170

"Do well in school, son," my Dad says to me. "That way nobody will bother you and you can go off and learn what you want." He grins at me.

I don't understand what he is talking about, but I guess he does. I am silent.

"Do you know what I mean?" he asks.

"Ah, sure, Dad. Sure," I say. What does he mean? That school isn't a place to learn. Hmm . . .

He smiles and pats me on the head.

In this example, the minor character, Dad, knows something the major central character doesn't know yet.

DIALOGUE — is what is spoken between two or more people. It will make any story more interesting. Believable dialogue is dialogue we can imagine the person saying.

DISTANCE, or distancing effect — is the feeling a reader has of being kept at arm's length from the events in the story and from the emotions of the central characters. Distance can be frustrating for the reader who wants to know and feel more about these events and characters. The past tense automatically creates a sense of distance. Too many adjectives or adverbs create distance. Intellectual and emotionless words create distance. Stiff, complicated sentences also create distance.

INTIMACY, or emotional intimacy — is the experience of knowing what the characters think and feel and of being able to see the events described so closely that the reader feels swept up in the action and feelings of the moment. Dialogue creates a sense of intimacy between the narrator and the other characters. Inner thoughts and feelings create a sense of knowing the narrator as if he or she were your own self.

INNER MONOLOGUE, or inner dialogue — is the words spoken inside the central character's head to himself or herself. For example: "Dad watches television all during dinner. 'I bet he won't even notice if I sneak some ice cream,' I think to myself." They add great richness to any story.

INNER WORLD — is the private world in which we all dwell much of the time. This world includes our joys, fears, and thoughts. Inner monologue, personal feelings, and thoughts create this picture.

NARRATIVE — is the unfolding of events in a way that holds the reader's interest.

NARRATOR — is the person who is telling the story. Sometimes it will be a character in the story, sometimes it will be someone outside the story looking down at the events as if he were God.

OUTER WORLD — is the public world of people and events that exists outside of ourselves. Dialogue and narrative are our tools to create pictures of the outer world.

PERSON — the story may be told in the first person ("I went to the market"), in the second person ("you went to the market"), or the third person ("she went to the market"). Most fiction is written in the third person; most effective life writing is done in the first person.

POINT OF VIEW — is the vantage point from which the story is being told. For example, during the nineteenth century the point of view was most often God-like and impersonal, allowing the writer to tell the reader directly what the atmosphere was like. ("It was a dark and gloomy night as Geronimo stood at the entrance to the cave looking in.") In the twentieth century, we tend to believe a story only if we know from whose point of view we are viewing the action. ("Geronimo stands at the mouth of the cave. 'It is very dark in there,' he says to himself. 'Dark as night.' He steps forward, inching his way into the blackness.")

SELF-CRITICISM — In our inner world, we often send messages to ourselves that tell us we are wrong, foolish, misguided, imperfect, and the like. Finding fault with ourselves causes us to feel badly about ourselves and causes us to stop doing the things we are doing.

SELF-DOUBT — is the disbelief we carry around about ourselves. We often do not believe we are good, capable, or caring people.

TENSE — or time. There are three basic times periods in which to set a story: the past, the present, and the future. In life writing we choose to narrate the story in the present rather than the past. To go into the past and then recreate that moment as if it were happening now creates a leap in the imagination of the writer and the reader. For example:

> It is 1963 and I am playing basketball in the gym of the USAF Academy. I hear over the loudspeaker: "Attention, attention. The president of the United States has been shot. His condition is not known." I am stunned and shocked.

In this way, the reader feels as if she or he has been carried from the present into another time and place. The reader is not looking back in time. The reader *is* back in time. When a writer goes into the past and recreates it using the present tense, the writer will usually recall much more of the event than if she or he were using the past tense.

VERBS — are where the actions in a story lie. Effective verbs arouse people's emotions. Powerful verbs are the strength of a story.

Appendix A

The Philosophy of Teaching "Writing from Within"

Writing from Within weaves together three disciplines: traditional literary elements, dramatic principles, and psychotherapeutic axioms. You as a teacher may be able to teach the materials more effectively by understanding where they come from.

Traditional Literary Elements

The traditional literary elements are characterization, plot structure, setting, point of view, language, imagery, theme, and style. By understanding these elements, one can analyze the works of writers from Shakespeare to Toni Morrison while appreciating them as well.

For many of you who come to the teaching of "writing from within" with a background in teaching English, your knowledge of these elements may be quite helpful. This expertise of yours may also be inhibiting; however, you may actually have to undergo a process of "unlearning" what you have held dear about writing for many years. I have found that well educated people often have to go through this unlearning process. As a teacher, bear in mind that most novelists and playwrights start with a germ of an idea, one based on an experience the writer has had, a person she or he has met, or a theme presented in a book, play, or film which the author has seen. Likewise, "writing from within" begins with the recollection of powerful moments, people, or places experienced in life. It is comparable to sketching from life; yet in almost every story there will also be a concern for the traditional literary elements—characterization, plot structure, setting, point of view, language, imagery, theme, meaning and style.

> *Characterization:* People are interesting, especially as their actions and behavior reveal different aspects of their characters. We try to reveal these different aspects through their thoughts, feelings, and actions.

> *Plot structure:* The mind can keep just so much information on hand and process it at one time. Structure helps us within this

processing of information. Certain things are included; certain things are left out; certain things are high-lighted and empha-sized.

175

The
Philosophy
of
Teaching
"Writing
from
Within"

Point of view: In an effort to bring the reader as close to the actual experience of the writer as possible, the writer enables the reader to see the world through his own eyes. For example, when the writer was a child, the reader will experience life as a child, when everything was fresh.

Language: As a writer gets back into a time when she was a child, the listener begins to hear distinct changes in language. These smaller sentences have an enormous impact on the listen-ers. When longer, adult words are used, the mood is broken, the connection to the picture severed, and belief strained.

Imagery: Those pictures that remain vivid in our minds for a long time seem to have a life of their own. When the king is killed in Macbeth, mother birds devour their young, horses rear up against their masters—a world order gone mad. A tortoise crawling across a sun-baked road at the beginning of *Grapes of Wrath* is struck by a passing car, flipped over on its back and left to die; a harbinger of what is to happen to the Joad family as they seek survival in California. These are powerful images, obviously images symbolic of the worlds in which the charac-ters function. In "writing from within," the writer shares vivid images from his own experiences with the reader. Because of the power of the written word or spoken word to create images, the first and most important task in recapturing these experi-ences is that the reader be able to see the experience in his mind.

Setting: Many important human experiences revolve around places as well as people, so these become separate writing assignments.

Dramatic Techniques

Actors, playwrights, and directors have a set of concerns which can be of great help to the teacher of life writing. Here are some I learned from Jack Garfein and Lee Strasberg.

1. Building the character

2. Defining prior circumstances

3. Working from moment to moment

4. Using sense memory

5. Uncovering the circumstances around an object

6. Finding the spine of the role and of the story or play

Constantin Stanislavski, the father of the "method" school of acting, writing, and directing, was concerned about overcoming sentimentality, melodrama, and "mood" in the acting and writing of his time. Sentimentality may be defined as the presence of overabundant emotion—particularly sweet or positive ones—where such emotion is not warranted. Thus, a long, grandiloquent speech extolling the beauty and virtue of a flower or a woman's nose may be termed sentimental. The character must "earn the right" to say what he or she is saying or feeling.

Melodrama may be defined as the presence of overabundant deep feelings, particularly negative ones, where such deep feelings are not warranted. Television cop shows in which murders occur early are examples of this. Typically, we see the victim's wife or girlfriend reacting very strongly; yet we are unable to feel deeply about the victim or the wife/girlfriend because we do not know them, or the potential killers, or even the cop. The situation is a life and death one, yet only a small range of their emotions and only a limited view of their characters are evident.

"Mood" acting means defining a moment in the play or film in terms of the overall feeling of the scene instead of creating the actions that will produce human emotions. For example, actor X reads through the play or script he has been given and decides that in a certain scene or passage he is angry or anguished or confused, whereupon he then attempts to act angry, anguished, or confused. This is called *mood* or *result acting*, which is taking the easy way out. It gives the audience a very general impression of what the character is experiencing, but there is nothing authentic or real about the character's responses to the circumstances of his life.

Sentimentality, melodrama, and mood acting pretty much defined the theater of Stanislavski's youth. He sought to find ways for the actor and writer to create on stage the most authentic circumstances within which the character would be compelled to take action—and the actors would be impelled to act.

In our work in life story writing, we want to accomplish the same thing. We want to develop stories devoid of sentimentality, melodrama, and vague, generalized, "moody" circumstances. We want our characters to be clear and well-rounded, with numerous, even contradictory, dimensions visible.

1. Building A Character

What a character wants out of life is his goal. What stands in his way are his obstacles. How he goes about overcoming his obstacles is his adaptation. What he finds deep within himself to help him adapt to his circumstances we call his character qualities—his charm, trustworthiness, cleverness, adaptability, tenacity, etc. These are the things that get him through life. Look at yourself and define in a word what you use to get yourself through life. In every circumstance, achieving a goal requires that we overcome obstacles. The actions we take to overcome these obstacles come directly from our character qualities as human beings.

2. Defining Prior Circumstances

The specific circumstances into which a person is born and in which she was raised, determine the character's goals, obstacles, struggles, adaptations, and actions. Yet the actor or playwright does not give us a lengthy explanation of these circumstances before the play opens. She allows them to unfold as the play develops. In helping people write their life stories authentically, I suggest to students they allow prior circumstances (i.e., what comes before the beginning of the story) to be told as the story develops. If more information needs to be given, it can be given when the drama is over.

3. Working Moment to Moment

To combat mood acting and sentimentality, Stanislavski instructed his players to work on each moment of the play as if they did not know what was coming next. For example, if one performer's objectives were too weak to keep his partner on stage, the partner was free to walk off stage. This improvisational, unexpected quality led to freshness. Actors were "in" their parts every moment. Likewise, in our writing, as a story comes to its climax the writer begins to expand the moment. That is, he or she lets us see more and more of what is happening from moment to moment.

4. Using Sense Memory

Giving the reader a sense of how things feel at the beginning, again in the middle, and at the end of a story helps: it may be cold outside, later warmer inside, then cool outside. We tend to stress sight above all else, yet sounds, touches, tastes, and smells may be even more powerful.

5. Exploring the Circumstances Surrounding An Object

As a way of building an environment in which he will be compelled to take actions, the actor will often surround himself with objects having very special meaning to himself. Familiar objects may have an enormous past attached to them and may cause us to feel very strongly. These objects may be a part of the actions a character takes. Such objects also help the writer get back to the situation(s) about which he is writing.

6. Finding the Spine

Each story has its own emotional logic, its own concerns; and the line of that logic is the spine. Anything else should be left aside. Other concerns, issues, and people need to be dealt with at a later time. Finding the spine, and then keeping to it, is closely related to structure. Since the mind can hold just so many things in it at one time, we have to limit the mind's attention to those things that are related to the spine.

Therapeutic Origins

Having paid attention to traditional literary elements and Stanislavski's approach to drama, we understand a bit better the origins of what "writing from within" life writing teachers teach. Now we need to pay attention to *how* it is best taught, through discussion of twentieth century therapeutic techniques.

Contributions of Gestalt Psychology

In life writing classes we learn to listen. Not only do we learn to listen carefully to events, but we also learn to listen to our own responses to what is being told us. We keep one ear open to what is being said outside ourselves and one ear open to how it resounds and feels inside ourselves. From gestalt psychology we learn to respond to the world with statements of how we feel—not with statements of right and wrong; not with "You shouldn't have done that . . . ," which is an intellectual, judgmental statement, but rather, "What you said hurts me . . . confuses me," etc. No one can argue with what you are feeling. This of course does not mean we say things such as "I feel you have gone off on the wrong track." Here 'feel' simply means "thinks" or "believes." As teachers we are asking the listeners to give statements of how they "feel," not what they believe or think. Learning to respond to stories using this kind of

feeling statement allows us to give others truly helpful feedback with
their stories.

179

The
Philosophy
of
Teaching
"Writing
from
Within"

Insights into the "Critic-Creator" Conflict

In Jungian psychology, we find much attention paid to the need for
balance between the often warring reactions of the masculine and
feminine sides of ourselves, between the analytical/critical vs. the
synthetic/creative sides of ourselves, and between the negative and
positives sides of ourselves. The positive sides of both masculine and
feminine have certain characteristics, as do the negative sides. We
can look at the *creator-critic* conflict in the same way.

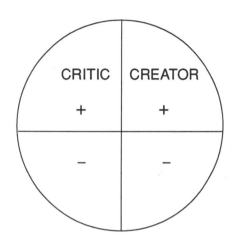

Let us now name a few characteristics of each side.

Critic	*Creator*
analytical	synthetic
logical	holistic
sequential	simultaneous
organized	organic
on track	off (a dull) track
piercing through (fluff)	imaginative
disdains the imaginative	jumbles
isolates	confuses
imposes structure on flow	defies order/reason

APPENDIX B

RECORDING ORAL HISTORIES

Students and children who wish to interview others need to ask questions that enable the persons being interviewed to reveal as much interesting information about themselves and their experiences as possible. I have therefore included a list of questions here to aid students. The questionnaire is followed by a sample oral history by Nat Leventhal.

Interview Questions

1. What is your earliest memory?

2. What is your earliest truly strong and powerful memory?

3. Can you describe your parents or the person(s) who raised you?

4. What were the strongest good and bad traits of your parents?

5. Do you remember any stories that illustrate these traits?

6. What is the happiest early memory you have?

7. What is the saddest or most frightening early memory you have?

8. What are some of the experiences you remember most vividly from your childhood?

9. Do you remember any friends who were particularly important to you?

10. Do you remember any interesting stories about these friends?

11. What was school like?

12. Do you remember any interesting stories about your schooling?

13. Who was the first boy (or girl) you fell in love with? What was that like?

14. Do you remember any difficult or important decisions you had to make during your early years?

15. What were some of the jobs or occupations you worked at during your life?

16. Do you remember any interesting or funny stories about your work?

17. Many times in life we remember things one way, but our friends and relatives remember them differently. Do you have any experiences like this?

18. Often in life we have stories of sadness and trauma that are important to talk about. What has happened in your life that you remember with real sadness?

19. Most of us have had one person in our lives who was very important to us, a man or woman whom we have loved a great deal. Who was that person in your life?

20. What was it about that person that made him or her so special?

21. How did you meet? What were the circumstances?

22. Were there other people—teachers, counselors, friends— who helped shape your life and attitudes?

23. Who were they? What were they like?

24. Many people have children who have given them a great deal of pleasure and pain. Would you like to describe yours?

25. Do you remember any stories that really tell something about your relationship with your children?

26. If there was one thing you could tell your children and those who will come after them, what would it be?

Oral Histories: An Example

The following oral history segment is a fragment from the life story of Nat Leventhal, an eighty-six-year-old former tailor who emigrated from Russia and was intimately involved with the growth of the garment industry in the United States from 1914 onward. He returned to Russia in the late 1920s to help Russian garment workers learn American garment industry techniques, some of which, paradoxically, he had learned in Russia as a small child.

Becoming an American
by Nat Leventhal
Interviewed and edited by Betty Springer

In July of 1914, I came to the harbor of Boston. Everything
looked so different to me. The people who were working at
the docks had hard straw hats and they spoke a language
which I couldn't understand; it was strange to me. They
didn't have quotas. They just looked at you and saw if you
were healthy, then they put you on a train and sent you
where you belonged. At that time the immigrants were
accepted with open arms, regardless of race, color, or whatever. Five doctors looked me over to make sure I was healthy
and then I was put on a train to Chicago. My sister lived in
America, and she had bought my tickets ahead of time and
made the arrangements with the agent. When we got to
Chicago she was waiting outside the station. There were no
guards and we walked among the Americans. She recognized
me and took me to her home on a streetcar. In those years
when I came, my sister had a grocery store in the front and
the living quarters in the back. She had a big galley stove that
used to keep us warm. We used to put coal in it and would
stay around the stove. We didn't have bathtubs in the house;
we went to the steam houses. We did not have toilets in the
apartment. They were in the hallway and everybody got a
key for the toilets. That was the life in those days, in 1914 and
1915. In those days when you came to a place on the Loop
between downtown and home you used to get a big stein of
beer for five cents, then all the smorgasbord you could eat
for free. That was those days! When I stayed with my sister,
I used to get a nickel and we'd get pails made out of metal
which would take about fifteen glasses of beer. We used to
go to the brewery and pick up a pail of this beer on hot days
in the summer. The whole family used to drink beer and that
was our enjoyment. When we had time on Sunday, we used
to go to a park near the lake. My sister would bring sand-
wiches and we used to have a good time. We also had in
Chicago the Jewish theater, the Jewish papers. We didn't have
to use the English language so much. Most of us used the
Jewish language at home, therefore we still retained our
accent. We hadn't developed a real American accent. Afterwards, I was trained to be a tailor. I first started to train when
I was six years old in Russia. In America I didn't know the
language, but I read the Jewish papers and found an ad for
a man that knows tailoring. So, I came to work early in the

morning, at seven o'clock. I did my work and at seven in the evening, I said, "I'm going home."

What's the matter with you, half a day? Seven to seven is half a day! So, I didn't want to work there any more.

At that time there were no automobiles but mostly horses and wagons. I used to try to learn to jump on the streetcar, to jump on and off. That was a trick that all the youngsters used to do. I did, too. But one time I got dressed to visit my sister about fifty miles away. I jumped off one street car to take the other, and jumped wrong. I jumped straight and fell in the mud. I was all covered with mud, and when I went to my sister, she didn't know who it was. Finally she recognized me. I had to change from head to foot because I was all smeared up.

This type of oral history has its advantages: simplicity and the relative ease with which the subject can tell his story. It has its disadvantages too. First, the story is almost always told by means of an uninterrupted narrative, with little or no dialogue or inner thoughts. The story is not shaped in any way. After a while, uninterrupted narrative becomes taxing, even boring for us to read. To hold our interest, stories need variety and contrast. Second, the teller of the story seldom does any rewriting of the story so the process of exploring one's own search for truth through revising is lost. Third, stories of an event may be well-told orally, but a story involving relationships often cries out for a fuller and deeper treatment of the experience using dialogue, inner monologue, and attention to form. Nevertheless where the storyteller does not wish to or cannot go into more depth, this type of oral history is viable and interesting.

Selected Readings

Writing Models

Aiken, Conrad. "Silent Snow, Secret Snow." In *The Collected Short Stories*. New York: Schocken Books, 1982.
"Silent Snow, Secret Snow" allows us to glimpse a young boy's fascinating and very private world from his point of view.

Bierce, Ambrose. *The Stories and Fables of Ambrose Bierce*. Owings Mills, MD: Stemmer House Publishers, 1977.
The stories "Occurrence at Owl Creek Bridge," "The Boarded Window," and "One of the Missing," provide superbly shocking, unpredictable, mind-teasing endings.

Campbell, Joseph. *Hero with a Thousand Faces*. Princeton, NJ: Princeton University Press, 1973. *The Masks of God* (4 volumes). New York: Penguin, 1970, 1976.
The path of the hero in everyone is traced through quests and temptations, weaving its way through virtually all of the world's mythologies and religions.

Doctorow, E. L. *World's Fair*. New York: Fawcett Crest, 1986.
Doctorow's novel, which displays a number of techniques of life writing, chronicles the events and experiences of his fictional hero's life.

Dostoevsky, Feodor. *Crime and Punishment*. New York: Bantam Books, 1984.
The author interweaves first person narrative, dialogue, and inner monologue in this classic story of risk-taking, crime, and conscience.

Dreiser, Theodore. *The Best Short Stories of Theodore Dreiser*. Chicago: Ivan R. Dee, Inc., 1989.
The narrator's voice in a Dreiser story is often clumsy and intrusive, a legacy of the nineteenth century, yet the stories are well worked out, and often gripping and ironic.

Hemingway, Ernest. *Collected Short Stories*. New York: Charles Scribners Sons, 1938.
Hemingway's narrator remains as discreet and inconspicuous as Dreiser's is heavy-handed. The author makes his points dramatically through dialogue and occasional inner monologue.

Ibsen, Henrik. *Complete Major Prose*. New York: New American Library, 1978.
The plot structure and problems Ibsen sets for his characters and the qualities he gives them make his plays forever interesting.

Lang, Fritz. *M*. (Classic Film Scripts, a series). London: Lorrimer Publishing, 1973.
In M, we experience the forcefulness of pursuers, including the protagonist's own conscience, from the point of view of the criminal pursued.

Miller, Arthur. *Death of a Salesman*. New York: Penguin, 1977.
The struggle of a character to achieve a goal and the way he pursues it when he cannot have what he really wants give Miller's play dignity and meaning.

O'Connor, Flannery. *The Complete Stories*. New York: Farrar, Straus and Giroux, 1971.
O'Connor offers some of the most bizarre and interesting characters in modern short stories.

Orwell, George. *Collected Essays* (4 volumes). San Diego: Harcourt Brace Jovanovich, 1968.
"Shooting an Elephant" is classic autobiographical writing: crisp narrative storytelling, a clear view of the objective world facing the writer, physical action, and reflection on the meaning of the actions one takes.

Pirandello, Luigi. *Plays*. Middlesex, England: Penguin Books, 1962.
Pirandello's plays bring us into a series of delightfully separate worlds in which each character is convinced his view of the real world is correct and each character manages to convince us he is right.

Writing Process

Capacchione, Lucia. *The Creative Journal*. Athens OH: Ohio University Press, 1979.

Clurman, Harold. *On Directing*. New York: Macmillan, 1983.

Goldberg, Natalie. *Writing Down the Bones*. Boston: Shambhala Publications, 1986.

Rico, Gabriele. *Writing the Natural Way*. Los Angeles: J. P. Tarcher, 1983.

Stanislavski, Constantin. *An Actor Prepares*. New York: Routledge Theater Arts, 1989.

Ueland, Brenda. *If You Want to Write*. Saint Paul, MN: Graywolf Press, 1987.

Autobiographical Writing

St. Augustine. *The Confessions of St. Augustine.* New York: Mentor Books, 1963.

Dillard, Annie. *An American Childhood.* New York: Harper and Row, 1987.

Scott-Maxwell, Florida. *The Measure of My Days.* New York: Penguin Books, 1979.

Simon, Kate. *Bronx Primitive.* New York: Harper and Row, 1983.

Simon, Kate. *A Wider World: Portraits in an Adolescence.* New York: Harper and Row, 1986.

Wiesel, Elie. *Night.* New York: Bantam Books, 1982.

Wilde, Oscar. "Confessions." In *Complete Writings of Oscar Wilde* (10 volumes). New York: Nottingham Society, 1907.

Guides To Autobiographical Writing

Kanin, Ruth. *Write the Story of Your Life.* New York: Hawthorne Dutton, 1981.

Keen, Sam, and Anne Valley Fox. *Telling Your Story: A Guide to Who You Are and Who You Can Be.* New York: Signet Books, 1973.

Hateley, B.J. *Telling Your Story, Exploring Your Faith.* St. Louis: CBP Press, 1985.

Moffat, Mary Jane. *The Times of Our Lives.* Santa Barbara, CA: John Daniel and Co., 1989.

Collections

Walker, Scott, ed. *The Graywolf Annual Three: Essays, Memoirs and Reflections.* Saint Paul, MN: Graywolf Press, 1986.

Zinsser, William, ed. *Inventing the Truth: The Art and Craft of Memoir.* Boston: Houghton Mifflin, 1987.

INDEX

"WRITING FROM WITHIN" RESOURCES

WRITING FROM WITHIN: A Unique Guide to Writing Your Life's Stories
by Bernard Selling

Any writer can create vivid autobiographical stories and life narratives using the techniques taught in this book, which are based on Selling's widely followed classes and workshops. This program enables everyone interested in writing, to explore their lives, rediscover forgotten experiences, and find out hidden truths about themselves, their parents, and their family histories.

"Anyone who has ever lost the opportunity to find out what really mattered to an important friend or relative will respond instantly to this book." *— BOOKLIST*

288 pages ... Paperback ... $12.95 ... Revised second edition

---

"WRITING FROM WITHIN" WORKSHOPS

WORKSHOPS FOR TEACHERS: Turning Life Experience into Vivid Stories

Most of our lives are spent putting distance between ourselves, our experience, our abilities, and our feelings. Bernard Selling's workshops show teachers how to help students overcome that distance.

In the workshop you will find your own authentic, passionate writer's voice and enable your students to find theirs. You will explore your inner critic and assist students in finding and calming theirs; learn an innovative approach to teaching language skills; and help students become aware of themselves using their stories as mirrors.

This writing approach is currently being used by the Los Angeles Unified School District Adult Division, and by the AWEC "at risk" program.

PUBLIC WORKSHOPS: From Fear to Self-Awareness through Vivid, Personal Writing

Self-assessment is important if we are to live fulfilled and meaningful lives. "Writing from Within" workshops teach a powerful mode of personal expression and self-awareness. They enables you to discover your authentic voice by teaching us to see and write through the eyes of our inner child.

In the day-long **Introductory Workshop,** participants face their fear of writing, find their earliest memories, learn the value of supportive feedback, and learn basic writing techniques. In the day-long **Advanced Workshop,** participants explore powerful memories throughout their lives, tell a story from several points of view, record a story told to the writer by someone else, and learn re-writing as an avenue to the truth of one's experience.

To receive more information about any of these workshops, please contact:
Bernard Selling
1722 Oak Drive, Topanga Canyon, CA 90290
(310) 455-3407

Send for our free catalog of books

BOOKS FOR SCHOOLS

BOOKS FOR TEACHERS

HUMAN RIGHTS FOR CHILDREN: A Curriculum Guide
by the Human Rights for Children Committee/Amnesty International

> The curriculum activities for children 3–12 in this guide illustrate the ten principles of the U.N. Declaration of the Rights of the Child teaches universal rights and encourages the development of self-worth, multicultural awareness, and empathy for others.
>
> *96 pages ... 12 illus ... Paperback ... $10.95 (spiral $12.95)*

THE UPROOTED: REFUGEES AND THE U.S. — A Resource Curriculum
by Human Rights Education Steering Committee/Amnesty International

> Awareness and sensitivity to the experiences of all people are crucial in education. This book promotes that awareness by exploring refugee experiences throughout history and in our own communities. Includes a bibliography, filmography, and the U.N. Declaration of Human Rights.
>
> *224 pages ... 18 illus ... Paperback ... $15.95 (spiral $22.95) ... Available October 1994*

101 MUSIC GAMES FOR CHILDREN: Fun and Learning with Rhythms and Songs by Jerry Storms

> Written especially for families and teachers, this lively and imaginative book presents more than 100 simple games using music that kids and adults can play together. The games are not competitive and are designed to help children develop an ear for sound, to nurture relationships, and to invite both adults and children to express themselves creatively.
>
> *160 pages ... 32 illus ... Paperback ... $9.95 (spiral $12.95) ... Available September 1994*

BOOKS FOR COUNSELORS & ADMINISTRATORS

HELPING TEENS STOP VIOLENCE: A Practical Guide for Educators, Counselors, and Parents by Allan Creighton with Paul Kivel

> Based on years of consultations and successful workshops, this is a manual can help in initiating classroom discussions about violence. Developed and written by individuals active in violence prevention training, it is an essential guide for helping teenagers find their way out of the cycles of abuse.
>
> *176 pages ... Paperback ... $11.95 (spiral $14.95)*

SCHOOL CRISIS MANAGEMENT: A Team Training Guide
by Kendall Johnson, Ph.D.

> Written for school professionals, this detailed guide gives specific procedures for managing crisis situations in schools, bridging the gap between theory and the real world of school operations. 78 full-page charts outline each area of discussion, and which may be reproduced.
>
> *192 pages ... 78 illus ... Paperback ... $19.95 (spiral $24.95)*

Prices subject to change without notice

BOOKS FOR TEENS & PARENTS

SAFE DIETING FOR TEENS: Design Your Own Diet, Lose Weight Effectively, Feel Good About Yourself by Linda Ojeda, Ph.D.

Linda Ojeda objectively outlines the dangers of bingeing, bulimia, anorexia nervosa and yo-yo dieting, and offers young women a positive alternative to fad diets. She takes a common sense "calories in, calories out" approach along with exercise, to keep weight down permanently. Appendices include a calorie count chart for typical teenager foods. *Includes a removable parents' guide.*
128 pages ... Paperback ... $7.95

RAISING EACH OTHER: A Book for Teens and Parents
by Jeanne Brondino and the Parent/Teen Book Group

Written and illustrated by teens and parents in their own words, this book is a dialogue between generations. Among the topics discussed are trust, freedom, responsibility, drugs, sex, religion, and more. RAISING EACH OTHER shows what unites and divides teens and their parents, and how, through communication, they can help each other learn, grow, and love.
160 pages ... Paperback ... $8.95

TURNING YOURSELF AROUND: Self Help Strategies for Troubled Teens
by Kendall Johnson, Ph.D.

A support book for young adults going through difficult times. It follows the stories of three young people—a bulimic, an alcoholic, and a relationship addict—through their problems and stages of recovery. Each chapter is followed by provocative questions and exercises that help the reader to explore deeper issues. *Includes a special guide for parents, teachers, or counselors.*
224 pages ... Paperback ... $9.95

FEELING GREAT: Reaching Out to the World, Reaching in to Yourself—Without Drugs by Nancy Levinson & Joanne Rocklin, Ph.D.

A highly positive book for teenagers who are facing the pressures of drug and alcohol use. It shows how the best "highs" come from being deeply involved in life and the world. Parents, teachers, and counselors will find it an invaluable resource for working with drug-related issues.
112 pages ... Paperback ... $7.95

A BOOK FOR EVERYONE

COMPUTER RESOURCES FOR PEOPLE WITH DISABILITIES
by Alliance for Technology Access

This new book shows how people with disabilities can use the latest computer technology to enhance their lives. It offers guidelines for defining needs, building a supportive team, and making the right decisions. It is a complete sourcebook of the technology that can be used at school, at work, or at home alongside other people with or without disabilities.
256 pages ... 39 illus ... Paperback ... $14.95 (spiral $19.95)

Order toll-free at 1-800-266-5592

ORDER FORM

NAME

ADDRESS

CITY/STATE   ZIP/POSTCODE

PHONE   COUNTRY (outside U.S.)

TITLE	QTY		PRICE	TOTAL
In Your Own Voice *(paper)*		@	$ 14.95	
In Your Own Voice *(spiral)*		@	$ 22.95	
Writing From Within		@	$ 12.95	
Computer Resources . . . *(paper/spiral)*		@	$	
Feeling Great		@	$ 7.95	
Helping Teens Stop Violence *(paper/spiral)*		@	$	
Human Rights for Children *(paper/spiral)*		@	$	
101 Music Games for Children *(paper/spiral)*		@	$	
Raising Each Other		@	$ 8.95	
Safe Dieting for Teens		@	$ 7.95	
School Crisis Management *(paper/spiral)*		@	$	
The Uprooted: A Curriculum *(paper/spiral)*		@	$	
Turning Yourself Around		@	$ 9.95	

Shipping costs:
*First book: $2.50
($6.00 outside U.S.)
Each additional book:
$.75 ($2.00 outside
U.S.)
For UPS rates and
bulk orders call us at
(510) 865-5282*

TOTAL
Less discount @_____%   (   )
TOTAL COST OF BOOKS
Calif. residents add sales tax
Shipping & handling
TOTAL ENCLOSED
Please pay in U.S. funds only

□ Check   □ Money Order   □ Visa   □ M/C

Card # _____ Exp date _____

Signature _____

Complete and mail to:
Hunter House Inc., Publishers
P.O. Box 2914, Alameda CA 94501-0914
Orders: 1-800-266-5592
Phone (510) 865-5282 Fax (510) 865-4295
□ Check here to receive our book catalog

IOV 7/94